RAW

FOOD • RECIPES

RAW
FOOD • RECIPES
No Meat No Heat

LYNELLE SCOTT-AITKEN

Green Frog Publishing

Commissioned by Deborah Nixon
Text: Lynelle Scott-Aitken
Photographer: Alan Benson
Stylist: Vicki Liley
Designer: Avril Makula
Project Coordinator: Bettina Hodgson
Production: Sally Stokes and Eleanor Cant

Legal deposit second quarter 2005
Bibliothèque nationale du Québec and the National Library of Canada
ISBN 2-89455-191-6

Green Frog Publishing is an imprint of Guy Saint-Jean Éditeur inc.
3154, boul. Industriel, Laval (Québec) Canada H7L 4P7
Tel. (450) 663-1777 • Fax. (450) 663-6666
E-mail: saint-jean.editeur@qc.aira.com Web: www.saint-jeanediteur.com

Printed and bound in Singapore

Cover photograph Spiced Vegetable Crisps, page 41

Contents

8 Introduction

12 Ingredients

18 Equipment

21 Step-by-step Sprouting

22 Breakfast

Bircher muesli with strawberries and hazelnuts • Compote of dried fruits with oat "yogurt" • Fruit and nut granola with pepita "milk" • Melon fruit salad with mint • Muesli with honey and almond milk

28 Snacks and Starters

Asparagus spears with soy and sesame • Belgian endive cups with gremolata • Broccoli with green olive and avocado dip • Celery root rémoulade with red bell pepper and chervil • Cucumber and long beans in chili peanut dressing • Fennel carpaccio with green olives • Fig and melon in port wine • Green and yellow beans with walnut sauce • Mixed marinated olives with herbs and celery • Spiced vegetable crisps • Spicy mixed nuts • Tomato-and-basil-stuffed mushrooms • Vegetable crudités with hummus • Vine leaves stuffed with pine nuts, currants and Swiss chard (dolmas) • Zucchini strips with charmoula

48 Soups

Ajo blanco (Spanish chilled almond and grape soup) • Arugula, walnut and Jerusalem artichoke soup • Avocado and corn soup with chili and cilantro • Chilled cucumber soup with red radishes • Creamed cauliflower soup • Tomato and mint "gazpacho"

56 Salads and Vegetables

Artichoke, celery and pine nut salad with thyme and lemon dressing • Baby leeks with green olive and caper tapenade • Beet and carrot salad with walnuts • Black olive, fig and

arugula salad • Bok choy with Asian mushrooms marinated in ginger soy dressing • Broccolini with fermented black beans • Carrot stick salad with cilantro and chili • Celery and red apple salad with walnuts and "mayonnaise" • Green apple and radicchio salad with almond dressing • Jerusalem artichoke and spinach salad with hazelnut dressing • Macerated lemon and tomato salad • Orange, red onion and olive salad • Pear, walnut and bitter greens salad • Pink grapefruit, fennel and red onion salad • Pistachio, celery and cucumber salad with dates • Radish, kohlrabi and daikon salad • Red and green cabbage and kale coleslaw • Rainbow bell pepper salad with capers and preserved lemon • Spinach leaf, orange and avocado salad with chickpea sprouts • Sprouted grain and bean salad with sesame lime dressing • Zucchini, eggplant and bell pepper ratatouille

88 Sweets

Banana and cinnamon "ice cream" with walnuts • Coconut and pineapple cream • Coconut granita with fruit salad • Peach mousse with pistachios and raspberries • Spiced stone fruits macerated in dessert wine

96 Sauces, Dressings and Condiments

Black olive tapenade • Cucumber raita • Dried tomato paste • Garlic-and-rosemary infused olive oil • Pestos (Basil and pine nut, Cilantro and peanut, Arugula and walnut, Tomato and almond) • Preserved lemons • Sauerkraut • Sun-dried tomatoes

104 Drinks

Campari and blood orange slushie • Cooling cucumber and mint drink • Mango and cardamom lassi

108 Index
112 Guide to Weights and Measures

Introduction

The first bite of a crisp red apple and the creamy richness of macadamia nuts; vibrant leafy greens and fragrant fresh herbs and spices; aromatic flower honey and sweet dried fruits—these are raw whole foods and most of us eat them regularly as part of a balanced diet. Some people feel so well and full of energy after eating such food that they consciously choose to eat foods that are raw anywhere from 50 to 100 percent of the time. A raw whole-food diet can be delicious, varied and nutritionally balanced, and the only limits are access to a broad range of seasonal fresh produce and the cook's imagination.

In this book you'll find plenty of "No Meat, No Heat" recipes using completely raw ingredients. However, to comply with the principles of the raw food movement, we have also included a number of recipes that use either the dehydration method or other low-temperature enzyme-preserving options.

Primarily eating raw food is not new. Before the discovery of applying heat to food, it's exactly the way our ancestors lived. More recently (but further back than we might think—in 1904's *Uncooked Foods and How to Use Them* by Mr. and Mrs. Eugene Christian) people were encouraged to liberate themselves from the demands of stoking a fire, and increase their health by consuming foods in their natural, most nutritionally complete state. These ideas are enjoying a resurgence as many food professionals and health advocates support the practice of preserving and consuming so-called living enzymes by eating whole foods in their raw or low temperature–preserved state.

Raw food followers believe that the living enzymes present in fresh food, necessary for healthy digestion and catalysts for the body's many metabolic reactions, survive through temperatures up to around 110°F (55°C). They therefore encourage the consumption of foods either not heated at all, or heated only up to this maximum temperature. The basic idea is that foods naturally contain the perfect enzymes for their digestion and that by destroying them, the body must produce its own not-so-perfect enzymes. In some instances, such as with nuts and seeds, raw foods require soaking in water to start the germination process and render their goodness digestible.

The general premise behind the current raw food movement is that high-temperature cooking and other methods of processing and refining destroy these beneficial living enzymes in food. Raw food advocates attempt to address this by eating unprocessed raw whole foods or by preparing them using such low-impact methods as dehydrating (or drying in a low-temperature oven), macerating and marinating, pickling, blending, fermenting and culturing, sun-drying, juicing, soaking and sprouting, or growing. Some raw food advocates allow and encourage the light steaming or blanching (immersion in boiling water for 1–3 minutes) of difficult to digest vegetables such as the cabbage family, and sprouted beans and grains, to increase the bioavailability of their nutrients. It may be that the application of gentle heat renders the nutrients in

The raw shopping list includes diverse fresh vegetables and fruits, nuts and seeds, as well as sprouted grains, beans and legumes, wine and some other types of alcohol, dried fruits, sea vegetables, edible flowers and their waters, herbs and spices, some sweeteners, oils and some types of vinegar. Technically, it could also include any product that has been marinated, fermented, pickled, brined, sprouted or dried at low temperature (such as in a dehydrator, in a low oven, or by the sun). After this point the line about which foods are acceptable raw foods in the current movement begins to blur. Raw honey (acceptable even though it is heated during processing to 130°F), agar-agar (which is freeze-dried), nonraw food such as aged vinegar and high-quality cocoa or chocolate are used in small amounts by some.

The broadest definition of raw foods would include milk, cheese and many other dairy products; cured or air-dried meats such as jerky, prosciutto and salami; cured fish and fish "cooked" in citrus juice or vinegar; and raw eggs such as are used in a classic mayonnaise. But for many people, the current movement is an extension of being vegetarian and they may therefore exclude obvious animal products such as meat, fish and poultry, as well as animal by-products such as dairy, eggs and honey. Other raw food followers may include small amounts of animal products from time to time, as they feel the need. In all cases, raw whole foods are preferred over processed foods.

some foods more available for digestion. This, as with many aspects of a raw food lifestyle, comes down to personal preference.

The nutrients in fresh foods are vulnerable to heat, light and time, which means that in addition to reducing the loss of nutrients and enzymes through cooking, care needs also to be taken to ensure that food is as fresh from harvest as possible. Ideally, this means either growing produce yourself or, more realistically for most, choosing regional produce in peak season when it is not only at its nutritional best, but also the least expensive. There is disagreement about making use of a freezer, but many raw food cooks do freeze fresh foods either to preserve them during a glut or prepare them for such dishes as ice cream or sorbet.

Once you start thinking about eating raw food it becomes essential to look at issues of how that food is produced, which brings up the question of organics. Organic produce is generally preferred by raw food advocates, as they also tend to be aware of the environment and concerned about the use of chemicals in food production and sustainable agricultural practices. While evidence that organic produce has a better nutritional profile is inconclusive, there is no doubt about what you will not be consuming when you eat certified organic produce: potentially harmful fertilizers, fungicides, pesticides and herbicides, and experimental genetically modified organisms (GMOs) and genetically engineered (GE) crops, all of which are banned by organic certifying organizations. That, along with the assurance that the land and other resources (such as precious water and fertile soil) employed in the growing of your fresh produce is being managed in a sustainable way, is surely enough to encourage most people for whom organic produce is an option to use it.

Some people who begin to eat raw may find they naturally consume less food yet have more energy, while others may find that nagging minor health or weight issues simply resolve themselves without much apparent effort. If you try it, perhaps your skin may even glow with good health while your moods may become calmer. But the true barometer of any new way of eating is how it affects you and your health personally, and the ease with which you adapt to it. For many people, switching to vegetarian or raw food eating is a sudden and lasting choice, but for many others a transition time during which the body gradually adjusts may be far more realistic. For some people, it is not unreasonable to spend a decade or longer in transition to healthful ways of eating.

In any case, forcing your body to adapt to a way of living it is not ready for is ill-advised. It may be that you currently eat a full range of cooked and raw vegetarian and animal products, so a first step may be to move towards a vegetarian diet that includes

some cooked foods before graduating to a raw food diet. Alternatively, you may decide to continue eating animal products but choose to eat only raw foods. Over time the need for animal products may naturally reduce and fall away completely, or you may always find some animal products beneficial. People who want to reduce the amount of animal products in their diet could start by eating lower and lower down the food chain, from red meat down to poultry, fish and then animal by-products. If you are already vegetarian and looking toward going raw, you may think it's impossible to live without bread. So to ease your body into the process you could start eating naturally leavened or rye bread, or nutritious sprouted wheat bread. The point is that true change on a sustainable level can take time, so don't rush it, and keep listening to what your body needs. Signs of resistance such as craving a lot of nuts or oils may indicate that you need to slow down. Eating raw may only ever be a habit some people adopt part-time.

This book contains recipes for anyone who simply wants a great variety of fresh and flavorsome ideas for salads and vegetables, as well as for followers of raw food principles and curious onlookers. The recipes do not contain meat, fish, poultry, eggs or dairy, and there are only a few instances where honey is used (vegans could easily replace it with an alternative raw sweetener). At the end of a few recipes there are suggestions for people who may choose to eat raw animal products (such as using raw-egg mayonnaise in place of the nut versions given). For people in transition from a cooked animal product-heavy diet, many of the savory dishes in this book could be supplemented with a small amount of animal product if necessary for balance. There are a

Or you can check online and see what's available for your area. Be guided by your taste buds and the integrity of the people whose business practice and produce you like.

Once you've found the very best fresh produce you intend to eat raw, it must be well washed. Use a wooden vegetable brush on any visible dirt and soak produce in a sinkful of cold water to which ¼ cup (2 fl oz/60 ml) apple cider vinegar has been added (or use a or vegetable wash from health food stores). This will remove any parasites and other unwanted micro-organisms. If you routinely use nonorganic produce, a stronger wash of food-grade hydrogen peroxide (also from health food stores) will help denature poison sprays as well. Drain and pat the produce dry, then store carefully to retain optimum freshness.

Place vegetables and fruits in plastic bags in the refrigerator and put fresh herbs in a glass of water in the refrigerator and use within a few days. Ideally, buy only what you need for the two or three days to come. When you come to use vegetables and fruits, be aware that pesticides concentrate in the skins, so you may prefer to peel nonorganic ones, even if (as in the case of apples) they are otherwise edible. Unfortunately, just below the skin is also where many vitamins and minerals concentrate, so these will also be lost. Peeling will also remove the unwanted nonsoluble wax coatings.

few recipes that suggest blanching or steaming certain vegetables, and these have alternatives where possible. In short, there are lots of simple, nutritious dishes for everyday enjoyment using ingredients that are easy to find and methods that are simple to follow.

The first step on the path to healthy eating is finding great-quality fresh produce. Most of the ingredients in this book can be found at a supermarket or in its health food section, and a few ingredients are easily found at health food or Asian stores. But that's just the beginning. What you also need to do is choose stores that have the best-quality, freshest produce. You may find it at a dedicated organic store, or by checking out the health food stores, Asian supermarkets, farms, farmers' markets and food cooperatives near you.

In the pages ahead you'll find myriad flavors, textures and taste combinations to dive straight into. You won't need to search high and low for obscure and unusual ingredients, and you won't need to spend money on expensive equipment or foods to get started. All you need is some basic kitchen skills, a healthy appetite and a passion for good food.

Ingredients

Beans and legumes: Beans, legumes, chickpeas (garbanzo beans) and lentils are staple foods in hot climates where they can be spread out in their seedpods to dry naturally. They can be soaked and sprouted, which renders their nutrients available for digestion (see page 21 for step by step sprouting guide). See also Sprouts (page 15).

Coconuts: In Southeast Asia and the Pacific islands, coconut palms yield food, building materials, firewood, eating utensils, ropes and mats. Green coconuts are full of refreshing and nutritious coconut water and high-protein sweet flesh, or "jelly," while mature coconuts yield rich coconut milk and coconut cream. These are easy to process fresh, and can be frozen in ice-cube trays for use in sweets and dressings.

Dried fruit: Fruits such as grapes, plums, figs, dates and apples are regularly sun- or air-dried in hot climates for use year-round. They are a staple raw food item, although you may wish to confirm that your preferred brand is not mechanically dried, which may be at higher temperatures, and that they have been processed without the addition of the preservative sulfur dioxide.

Edible flowers: The use of fresh flowers in different edible preparations varies from culture to culture, with roses probably the most extensively used. Nasturtiums, marigolds (calendula), violets, rose petals and flowering herbs such as chives, rosemary, dill and basil are colorful and flavorful ingredients. Used sparingly, they can immediately dress up a simple salad or vegetable dish, and may also be steeped in drinks or vinegar for flavoring. Saffron and cloves derive from dried flowers. Pesticides concentrate in flowers, so use only organic or unsprayed ones from an unpolluted area.

Flower waters: Rose water and orange-blossom water are extensively used in Middle Eastern and Sub-continental dishes, and they can add an instant lift to fruit-based sweets, salads or drinks and are especially well matched with nuts such as pistachio and almond. Flower waters are an inexpensive and fragrant addition to the raw food pantry.

Grasses: Wheat is not the only grain that can be grown into chlorophyll-rich grass. Try sprouting and growing buckwheat greens and barley grass for variety. Wild rice, the seed of an aquatic grass, is also excellent sprouted and grown into grass.

Herbs and spices: Fresh herbs are preferable for raw food preparation, as many of the more delicate leaves such as parsley, basil, mint and chervil lose their fragrance when dried. Rosemary and thyme are pungent enough to withstand drying, but fresh is still best. The flavor of spices is not compromised by drying, and is sometimes intensified by it. Purchase small amounts of spices from a supplier with a high turnover, they will lose their pungency over time.

Honey: The flavor and nutrients of honey are easily destroyed by heat, so raw honey, which is heated during processing to an acceptable level, is the preferred choice in a raw food diet (other honeys are pasteurized). Apart from sugars and other substances in honey, there are enzymes, proteins, vitamins and minerals, which vary according to the nectar collected from a multitude of different flowers. Do not feed honey, raw or pasteurized, to children less than one-year old; the honey can contain bacteria that can lead to infant botulism. The more advanced immune systems of older children eliminate this danger.

Miso: Miso is a high-protein paste made from fermented soy beans, barley or rice. Lighter-colored miso has spent less time fermenting and is thus sweeter and milder in flavor. Darker miso has a longer fermentation time of up to three years, and is malty and intensely flavored. It is used as a seasoning in dressings, soups and pickles in ways similar to soy sauce. Because of its active cultures, miso is considered a "live" food, despite the fact that the beans it is based on are cooked before being mashed, salted and fermented.

Mushrooms: There is an extraordinarily diverse range of mushrooms suitable for eating. Mushrooms do not generally need washing. A gentle wipe with a dry cloth is sufficient to remove any dirt. Edible mushrooms should, however, be lightly steamed, dried, brined, pickled or marinated before eating to neutralize possible toxins. Lemon juice or vinegar can be used for marinating. Mushrooms not specifically identified as edible should never be consumed, as many types contain deadly toxins.

Mustard: Originally, mustard was made by mixing the crushed hot-tasting seeds (black, brown, white or yellow) of certain members of the cabbage family with unfermented grape juice (must). They are now more likely to be mixed with vinegar, and perhaps other spices depending on the style being made. Not all mustard is heated during processing, so check around for a raw source if you like this prepared flavor. Mustard can be smooth or contain half-crushed seeds. Mild Dijon is made from a combination of black and brown seeds while American-style mustard is made from milder white seeds. Mustard greens and mustard cress are also terrific in salads.

Nuts: Nuts are an excellent source of protein and energy, and the diverse range available means there are infinite ways to use them. It would be easy to overuse nuts in the early stages of eating raw food, so be mindful that they can be used in small quantities to provide flavor and texture rather than dominate some of the simpler dishes. Unshelled or whole nuts are best for freshness, otherwise find a supplier with a high turnover and don't buy too many nuts at once. This is especially important with walnuts, which become bitter over time. Blanched almonds have been boiled to loosen the skins for peeling, but the same can be achieved by soaking almonds overnight in water and peeling the skins off the next day. As with all nuts, soaking overnight in water starts the germination process, which increases the digestibility of their nutrients. Please note that some nuts may be heat-processed, so you may wish to check with your supplier that the nuts you are buying are raw.

Oils: There are a number of ways to extract oil from foods, including cold pressing, expeller pressing and solvent extraction, but the process used by any particular manufacturer does not need to be labeled on the finished product. Cold-pressed olive, flaxseed, grapeseed, hemp, raw sesame and nut oils are recommended, but you may need to confirm with the manufacturer that the oil, subsequent to cold pressing, was not subjected to heating, bleaching, degumming or other refining process that can compromise its nutritional value. Look for oils packaged in dark glass bottles in the refrigerator section of your health food store. Refrigeration indicates a short shelf life, suggesting less processing and maximum nutrient retention. Extra virgin olive oils are also an excellent choice.

Pepper: Black pepper is obtained by sun-drying the green berries of *Piper nigrum* until they become black and shriveled, which also intensifies their flavor. For dishes in which you prefer not to see black specks (such as white cauliflower soup), use milder white pepper. White pepper is made by soaking green berries in water to remove the outer skins and expose the paler center. These are then sun-dried until white and ready for use. Always grind pepper as you need it to preserve aroma and pungency. A hand-operated coffee grinder is ideal.

Salad leaves: Myriad types of lettuce, endive, radicchio, sorrel and bitter greens such as dandelion and watercress ensure infinite salad variations in a raw food diet. Although salad leaves are mainly water, they also contain good amounts of nutrition, especially the darker outer leaves.

Seaweed: Sea vegetables, or seaweed, are excellent as a flavoring or textural component to many dishes, especially those with an Asian influence. Types of edible seaweed include wispy arame, nori sheets for sushi, and wakame. They are usually sold dried and can be reconstituted by soaking in cold water before using in salads or dressings or, with nori, by simply breaking it up or filling and rolling vegetable sushi. Seaweed is an excellent source of minerals. Some seaweed is tough and requires cooking, so stick with these more tender types.

Sesame and tahini: Sesame seeds are high in calcium, in either their seed form or as sesame paste, known as tahini. They range from white to black, but ensure that regardless of color, you are buying raw and not toasted sesame seeds and tahini made from them. Dark sesame oil is made from toasted seeds, and is therefore not raw.

Sprouts: Fresh sprouts are remarkably nutritious and significantly expand the options of raw food advocates. Seeds, legumes and grains such as chickpeas (garbanzo beans), mung beans, alfalfa seeds, lentils, adzuki beans and wheat berries are all easy to sprout at home over a three- to four-day period. Only use whole seeds and beans, as split ones will not sprout. Sprouts grown from seeds are lighter and faster to sprout. See page 21 for step-by-step sprouting guide. Alternatively, look for sprouts at the supermarket.

Soy sauce: True soy sauce is a naturally fermented product made from soybeans, other grains and starter cultures. Some soy sauces are made with roasted

cracked wheat, which some raw food followers ignore because the soy becomes a "live food" through the fermentation process. Japanese tamari is wheat free, while nama shoyu is unpasteurized, which means it is not heated in manufacture.

Sun-dried sea salt: There are three main types of salt: table, rock and sea. Many salts are chemically- or heat-processed at staggering temperatures that destroy all mineral content, but sun-dried salts are also easy to source and full of minerals and flavor. Natural sea salts made from seawater (including Celtic, Lima, fleur de sel, Si and Maldon) will be labeled sun-dried. Sun-drying preserves the mineral content and the result is a gray, slightly moist salt with wonderful flavor.

Sweeteners: White sugar is highly refined, which means it doesn't figure in the raw kitchen. Instead, choose evaporated cane juice (not to be confused with cane sugar), which is sugarcane that has been juiced and dehydrated into granules and looks much like raw sugar. Date sugar is made from ground dried dates and, while it doesn't dissolve very well, it is excellent in breakfast cereals and fruit dishes. Pure maple syrup, the unrefined sap of the sugar maple tree, while not strictly raw has been heated far less than sugar and contains many nutrients. Likewise organic blackstrap molasses, while not strictly raw, is an unrefined by-product of sugar processing that contains plenty of minerals. Stevia is a sugar-free plant that is hundreds of times sweeter than sugar, and with none of sugar's negative effects. Look for it at health food stores and use very sparingly to supplement the effect of other sweeteners.

Vinegar: There are a number of flavorsome vinegars that will add variety to raw dishes. As they are so diverse, it is a good idea to experiment before choosing favorites. For Asian-inspired dishes there are Chinese and Japanese rice vinegars, while Mediterranean dishes are good with apple cider, red or white wine, aged balsamic, sherry, or fruit vinegars such as raspberry. In the case of wine vinegars, look for ones that are made from good-quality grapes. At the health food store look for umeboshi plum vinegar, the pickling liquid from umeboshi plums, which has a wonderful tangy, sour taste. Vinegar can be intensely acidic, so use it sparingly to heighten flavor.

Water: Fresh, pure water is a natural complement to raw food. Try to ensure that your drinking water, and water used to prepare foods such as nut milks and soups, is from a good source. Some options are certified organic, purified or filtered water. If you are concerned about losing the benefits of sodium fluoride in the city water supply (often added to increase the health of teeth), you can include more natural sources of fluorine in your diet by eating seaweed, cabbage, parsley, avocado and black-eyed peas.

Wine and other alcohol: Happily for many, wine is a raw food. Made by fermenting the juice of crushed grapes according to local tradition and practice, wine complements a raw food diet. Strict vegetarians may want to confirm that their wine is not fined with an animal product such as egg white. Fortified wines are higher in alcohol, while aperitifs and digestifs can be either wine- or spirit-based and flavored with secret herbs and spices. Small amounts, used almost as a "seasoning" in sweet dishes can transform them.

Equipment

Blenders: The three most common varieties are the regular stand blender, the high-speed blender, and the stick blender, also known as an immersion blender. The high-speed blender churns through tough nuts and raw vegetables to render them utterly smooth for flawless nut-based dressings, milks and raw soups. A slower blender will not be able to achieve the same result, which means the mixture may need to be strained and nutrition lost. Ensure the blender's blades are kept sharp, or replace them as needed with new ones. The stick blender is a useful and inexpensive tool for blending liquids that do not need to be perfectly smooth, such as some dressings and soups like gazpacho.

Cheesecloth (Muslin): Cheesecloth is useful for straining nut and seed milks and for covering the mouths of jars used to sprout seeds, beans and legumes. If it is washed well, it can be reused.

Cutting boards: Unfinished wooden cutting boards are ideal for food preparation, needing just a thorough washing and drying between uses. They are kinder to knives than plastic boards, which do not give during chopping. Keep a separate board for pungent ingredients such as onions, garlic and chili, or be sure to use just one side. Milder ingredients, such as fruits, will otherwise pick up some of the pungent residue.

Dehydrator: A dehydrator is a low-temperature "oven" that may be a plastic unit with colander-like trays, or it may look more like an oven with a fan for circulation and thermostat control. It can be expensive, so it's a good idea to experiment with low-temperature cooking in your domestic oven first. Use the bottom shelf of your oven with the temperature knob turned down below the markings and regulate the temperature with a thermometer.

Food processor: This is an essential tool for crushing nuts, whizzing frozen bananas into smooth ice cream, and preparing pastes such as pesto, which should retain some texture rather than being pureed until smooth. The slicer attachment makes short work of cabbage for coleslaw, and the grater is handy for carrots.

Japanese vegetable slicer or mandoline: Ideal tool for slicing fruits and vegetables wafer thin or into julienne, which looks good and can help the ingredients break down in dressings to aid digestion. It also reduces the pressure on your knife skills. Always use the hand guard to reduce the chance of injury.

Juicers: To juice citrus fruit for dressings, a simple wooden reamer is ideal. For larger quantities (such as for drinking fresh orange juice), a small electrical countertop version is useful. For very large amounts, or to make non-citrus juices, a more substantial countertop electric juicer is the best option.

Kitchen scales: Raw food cooking is not as precise as pastry making, but scales will allow you to keep an eye on the consumption of energy-dense nuts by weight, rather than volume. Some electronic scales also convert metric to imperial (and vice versa) of both solids and liquids, which is handy when you're making recipes from lots of different sources.

Knives: Varying the shape and thickness of ingredients is one of the ways to keep raw foods interesting, so a good selection of well-maintained knives is essential. Start with a chef's knife. It will bear the brunt of slicing, dicing and chopping, so be sure to get a good brand with a handle to suit your grip. A couple of small, sharp paring knives are the next most useful, as well as a small serrated knife.

Oven thermometer: This inexpensive piece of equipment allows you to check that the temperature of your oven is correct, and means you can turn the dial down below the numbers marked to the low temperature required for raw foods. Most ovens have warm and cool spots, so move the thermometer around to find the best and most evenly heated place for low-temperature cooking.

Vegetable scrubbing brushes: Choose a wooden brush with natural bristles for scrubbing dirt and debris from fruits and vegetables before preparing. In various sizes, the brushes just need a quick rinse under the cold tap and to be left out to dry in between uses to render years of service.

Step-by-step sprouting

1. Cover beans, grains or legumes with cold water and set aside at room temperature overnight.

2. Next day, rinse and drain well, place in a widemouthed jar covered with cheesecloth (muslin), and lay jar on its side.

3. Alternatively, place rinsed and drained grains, beans or legumes on a plate or tray lined with damp paper towels inside a plastic bag.

4. Set aside at room temperature for 3 days, taking care to rinse sprouts morning and evening.

5. When ready, the grain, bean or legume shoots will be up to 1 inch (2.5 cm) long.

6. Store prepared sprouts in the refrigerator for up to 3 days.

Breakfast

BIRCHER MUESLI
WITH STRAWBERRIES AND HAZELNUTS

½ cup (2 oz /60 g) unpeeled almonds, soaked
   overnight in cold water and peeled
1½ cups (12 fl oz/375 ml) tepid water
pinch sea salt
½ cup (2 oz/60 g) rolled oats
1 tablespoon flax seeds (linseeds)
½ teaspoon orange zest (optional)
1 tablespoon raw honey, plus extra to serve
1 cup (4 oz/125 g) strawberries, hulled and
   quartered
¼ cup (1½ oz/45 g) coarsely chopped hazelnuts

To make almond milk, blend peeled almonds, tepid
water and salt in a blender until smooth. Mix
unstrained almond milk with oats, flax seeds, zest
and honey, then cover and refrigerate overnight. Next
day, stir well and serve topped with strawberries,
hazelnuts and a drizzle of honey.

Serves 2

Note Peeled almonds are available, however they will
have been blanched in boiling water and are
therefore not strictly raw. This method of soaking
overnight in cold water not only loosens almond
skins, it also starts the germination process to
increase their digestibility.

Variation If you are pressed for time or do not want
to peel almonds, the equivalent quantity of pepitas
(pumpkin seeds) can be substituted. They also
benefit from overnight soaking to start the
germination process.

COMPOTE OF DRIED FRUITS WITH OAT "YOGURT"

4 oz (125g) dried figs, finely sliced

4 oz (125g) dried apricots or peaches, finely sliced

4 oz (125g) pitted dates, halved lengthwise

4 oz (125g) dried vine fruits such as raisins, currants or golden raisins (sultanas)

2 strips lemon peel, each ½ inch (1 cm) wide

2 strips orange peel, each ½ inch (1 cm) wide

1 cinnamon stick or 1 teaspoon ground cinnamon

1 vanilla bean (pod), seeds scraped

2 tablespoons lemon juice

1 tablespoon raw honey

1½ cups (12 fl oz/375 ml) water

1 cup (4 oz/125 g) rolled oats

½ teaspoon unpasteurized soy sauce (such as nama shoyu) or lemon juice

¼ cup (1 oz/30 g) coarsely chopped unpeeled almonds

Toss dried fruits, citrus peel, cinnamon, vanilla seeds and bean, lemon juice, honey and ½ cup (4 fl oz/ 125 ml) water together. Cover and set aside in a cool place (not the refrigerator) overnight. To make yogurt, blend remaining 1 cup (8 fl oz/250 ml) water with oats and soy until very smooth. Pour into a ceramic bowl and cover but do not seal (a piece of cheesecloth/muslin works well). Set aside in a warm place to ferment for up to 10 hours until your preferred level of sourness is achieved. Seal and refrigerate until cold. Next day, serve chilled yogurt over bowls of compote and top with almonds.

Serves 4–6

Note Nondairy yogurt may also be made from almonds (see page 107) or sunflower seeds. To speed fermentation next time you make it, use a few teaspoons of yogurt from the previous batch. It keeps well in the refrigerator for a few days after fermentation.

FRUIT AND NUT GRANOLA WITH PEPITA "MILK"

1 cup (4 oz/125 g) rolled oats

2 tablespoons sunflower seeds

2 tablespoons flaxseeds

¾ cup (4 oz/125 g) pepitas (pumpkin seeds)

½ cup (2½ oz/80 g) coarsely chopped mixed nuts

2 tablespoons muscat raisins (muscatels)

½ cup (3 oz/90 g) dried apricots, finely sliced

2 tablespoons raw honey or blackstrap molasses

2 teaspoons neutral cold-pressed vegetable oil
    such as flaxseed

1 cup (8 fl oz/250 ml) tepid water

pinch sea salt

Toss oats together with sunflower seeds and flaxseeds, ¼ cup (1½ oz/45 g) pepitas, mixed nuts, muscatels and apricots. Mix in honey and oil and continue to mix until ingredients are well coated and sticky. Spread the mix out on a dehydrator sheet or nonstick baking sheet and dry out either in a dehydrator or oven set to 110°F (55°C). The process may take 6–12 hours. While granola is drying, soak remaining ½ cup (2½ oz/80 g) pepitas in enough cold water to cover and set aside. When granola is crisp and dry, remove from the dehydrator or oven and set aside to cool. Store in an airtight container. To serve, drain pepitas and discard soaking water. Blend with tepid water and salt until very smooth. Either strain or serve as is over granola.

Serves 2–4

Note This recipe can easily be multiplied to make sufficient quantities for up to 1 month.

Variation As an alternative to pepita milk, try almond milk (see page 27) or serve with or without oat or seed yogurt (see page 24). If you want to change the mix, experiment with different combinations of seeds, nuts and dried fruits.

MELON FRUIT SALAD WITH MINT

1 cup (4 oz/125 g) honeydew melon balls

1 cup (4 oz/125 g) cantaloupe (rockmelon) balls

1 cup (4 oz/125 g) watermelon balls

1 tablespoon raw honey

1 teaspoon finely grated ginger

2 teaspoons finely chopped mint

½ cup (2 oz/60 g) raspberries

½ cup (2 oz/60 g) seedless black grapes, halved
    lengthwise

Gently toss melon balls, honey and ginger together and set aside for 20 minutes for the flavors to mingle. Fold in remaining ingredients and serve in chilled fruit bowls or glasses.

Serves 4

Variation To transform this into a quick and easy dessert, omit the honey and ginger and gently toss the fruit with a generous splash of dessert wine. Serve in frosted glasses garnished with fresh mint.

MUESLI WITH HONEY AND ALMOND MILK

¾ cup (3 oz/90 g) rolled oats

2 tablespoons oat bran

1 tablespoon flaxseeds

½ tablespoon unhulled sesame seeds

1 tablespoon pepitas (pumpkin seeds)

1 tablespoon sunflower seeds

3 tablespoons coarsely chopped nuts such as
    Brazil, hazelnut and/or almond

2 tablespoons chopped dried apricot or peach

2 tablespoons chopped dried apple or pear

2 tablespoons dried vine fruits such as raisins,
    currants and/or golden raisins (sultanas)

½ cup (2 oz/60 g) unpeeled almonds, soaked
    overnight in cold water and peeled

2 cups (16 fl oz/500 ml) tepid water

pinch sea salt

2 teaspoons raw honey, pure maple syrup or
    blackstrap molasses (optional)

To make muesli, mix together oats, bran, seeds, chopped nuts and fruits and store in an airtight container for up to a month. To make almond milk, blend peeled almonds, tepid water and salt until very smooth and either strain first or serve as is. Serve milk over muesli with a drizzle of honey if desired.

Serves 2–3

Variation Try different combinations of dried fruits, nuts and seeds, or serve muesli with chopped fresh fruits such as apple, strawberries or banana.

Snacks and starters

ASPARAGUS SPEARS WITH SOY AND SESAME

2 tablespoons unpasteurized soy sauce (such as
   nama shoyu)
1 clove garlic, crushed
½ bird's eye chili, seeded and finely diced
2 tablespoons cold-pressed sesame oil
freshly ground black pepper
1 lb (500 g) slender asparagus spears, fibrous ends
   trimmed
3 oz (90 g) garlic chives, about 1 bunch
1 tablespoon unhulled sesame seeds
1 lime, cut into 4 wedges

Mix together soy, garlic, chili and sesame oil and
season to taste with pepper. Bring a pan of water to a
boil; remove from heat, plunge asparagus spears into
water and set aside for 2 minutes, or steam over a
pan of boiling water for 2 minutes. After 2 minutes,
add garlic chives for 20 seconds, then drain
altogether. Toss asparagus and garlic chives in
dressing, then add sesame seeds. Transfer to serving
plates and serve with a wedge of lime to the side.

Serves 4

Note If you prefer not to blanch or steam asparagus,
simply cut spears into fine slices on the extreme
diagonal before tossing through dressing. Reduce
garlic chives by half, and cut into 1 inch (2.5 cm)
lengths before adding to asparagus.

BELGIAN ENDIVE CUPS WITH GREMOLATA

For the gremolata
zest of 2 lemons
2 cloves garlic, crushed
⅔ cup (⅔ oz/20 g) coarsely chopped parsley
sea salt
freshly ground black pepper
¼ cup (2 fl oz/60 ml) extra virgin olive oil

16 unblemished Belgian endive leaves
2 oz (60 g) pea shoots
1 English (hothouse) cucumber, peeled and cut
    into 48 even strips (to match the bell pepper)
1 medium red bell pepper (capsicum), seeded
    and cut into 24 even strips
1 medium yellow bell pepper (capsicum), seeded
    and cut into 24 even strips

To make gremolata: Place lemon zest, garlic and
parsley in a bowl and season with a pinch each of salt
and pepper. Stir in the olive oil and check seasoning;
the mix will be very pungent.

Arrange the endive leaves on a serving platter in a
single line in a top-and-tail manner. Place a few pea
shoots, 3 strips of cucumber, then 3 strips of red bell
pepper in an endive leaf and place a spoonful of
gremolata on base of leaf and its contents. With next
leaf, repeat process using yellow bell pepper instead
of red. Continue alternating red and yellow strips
along endive leaf line until all ingredients are used.
Serve immediately as an appetizer with drinks.

Makes 16

Variation To increase the energy of these morsels,
place slender strips of ripe avocado in cups along
with other ingredients. If you do not intend to serve
them immediately, be sure to toss the avocado slices
gently in lemon juice before preparing the dish to
slow oxidization.

BROCCOLI WITH GREEN OLIVE AND AVOCADO DIP

2 large, ripe avocados, pits and skins removed

½ cup (3 oz/90 g) pitted green olives

2 cloves garlic

1 red chili, seeded and finely chopped

2 tablespoons lime or lemon juice

3 tablespoons extra virgin olive oil,
    plus 1 teaspoon for dressing

sea salt

freshly ground black pepper

¼–½ cup (2–4 fl oz/60–125 ml) water

14 oz (440 g) broccoli or broccolini, about
    1 head or 2 bunches

In a food processor, place avocado flesh, olives, garlic, chili and lime juice and blend until smooth. Slowly add 3 tablespoons olive oil and season to taste with salt and pepper. The thickness of the mixture will vary, so add just enough water to make a good dipping consistency. Cover tightly with plastic wrap, pressing plastic down onto the surface of the dip to prevent oxidization. Trim broccoli ends and cut larger pieces in half lengthwise. Bring a pan of water to a boil, remove from heat, immerse broccoli in water, set aside for 2 minutes and then drain; or steam over a pan of boiling water for 2 minutes. Toss in 1 teaspoon olive oil and season with salt and pepper. Serve with a bowl of dip to the side or drizzle dip over the top.

Serves 2–4

Note Some followers of raw food principles believe that gentle steaming or blanching of vegetables that are difficult to digest increases the availability of their nutrients. If you prefer not to steam or immerse your vegetables in boiling water, substitute ones that are more pleasant to eat raw, such as cauliflower, carrots, celery, young peas and cucumbers.

Variation Try broccoflower, a cross between broccoli and cauliflower, for a change.

CELERY ROOT RÉMOULADE WITH RED BELL PEPPER AND CHERVIL

½ cup (2 oz/60 g) pine or macadamia nuts, soaked
    in water for 6 hours
2 tablespoons lemon juice
1 teaspoon smooth or mild mustard, such as Dijon
¼ cup (2 fl oz/60 ml) extra virgin olive oil
2 tablespoons water
1 clove garlic, crushed
sea salt
freshly ground black pepper
1 medium (1 lb/500 g) celery root (celeriac)
6 garlic chives or ½ bunch regular chives
Belgian endive leaves or radicchio cups
1 small red bell pepper (capsicum), seeded and cut
    into very fine julienne
¼ cup (1 oz/30 g) chervil sprigs

Drain nuts and discard soaking water. Blend with lemon juice, mustard, olive oil, water and garlic until smooth. Season to taste with salt and pepper and set aside. Working as quickly as is safely possible, trim celery root stalks and peel thickly to remove skin. Cut into very thin slices, stacking slices as you go. Once root is cut, cut slices into very fine julienne and immediately toss with dressing, as pieces will oxidize after just a few minutes. Stir garlic chives through the mix and serve in cups of radicchio or Belgian endive on either individual serving plates or a platter. Top with bell pepper julienne and chervil and serve immediately.

Note Some followers of raw food principles include raw eggs in their diet. In this case, 1 cup (8 fl oz/250 ml) classic mayonnaise made with raw egg yolks, mustard, lemon juice and extra virgin olive oil may be substituted for the nut "mayonnaise" dressing.

Serves 2–4

CUCUMBER AND LONG BEANS IN CHILI PEANUT DRESSING

1 shallot (French shallot), finely chopped

½ tablespoon pure maple syrup

2 tablespoons rice vinegar

1 bird's eye chili, seeded and finely sliced

1 tablespoon chopped cilantro (fresh coriander) stems

1 lb (500 g) long (snake) beans, trimmed, cut into 2-inch (5-cm) lengths

⅓ cup (3 oz/90 g) chopped peanuts

1 English (hothouse) or 3 small Lebanese cucumbers, peeled, seeded and cut into chunks

sea salt

freshly ground black pepper

¼ cup (¼ oz/7 g) cilantro (fresh coriander) leaves, to garnish

Mix together shallot, maple syrup, rice vinegar, chili and cilantro stems and set aside. Bring a pan of water to a boil and remove from heat. Plunge beans into the water and set aside for 3 minutes, or steam over a pan of boiling water for 3 minutes. Drain well and toss through chili mixture. Add peanuts and cucumber and toss to combine. Season with salt and pepper to taste, then serve with scattered cilantro leaves.

Serves 4

Note Long beans are a bit tough to eat raw, so if you prefer not to blanch or steam any vegetables, replace the long beans with tender, young green beans. To prepare them, trim stem ends and slice thinly lengthwise before tossing in chili mix. Leave them in chili mix for 30 minutes or so to soften slightly before continuing with the recipe.

FENNEL CARPACCIO WITH GREEN OLIVES

1½ tablespoons sherry or white wine vinegar
2 cloves garlic, crushed
½ teaspoon crushed fennel seeds
¼ cup (2 fl oz/60 ml) extra virgin olive oil
sea salt
freshly ground black pepper
2 medium bulbs (about 1⅓ lb/650 g total) fennel,
    fronds attached
¼ cup (1¼ oz/45 g) pitted green olives, cut into
    very fine strips

In a large bowl, mix together vinegar, garlic, fennel seeds and olive oil and season to taste with salt and pepper. Trim fennel bulbs, reserving enough fronds to yield 1 tablespoon when finely chopped. Remove any coarse outer layers from fennel. Keeping them in a whole piece, place base of a bulb on a Japanese vegetable slicer or mandoline and finely slice. Repeat with remaining bulb and gently toss through dressing. Layer slices onto serving plates, cover and set aside for ½–1 hour for fennel to soften. When you're ready to serve, scatter sliced olives and chopped fennel frond on dressed fennel and serve.

Serves 4

Variation Try adding ½–1 tablespoon chopped nonpareil (baby) capers to the dressing, or serve a bowl of pink grapefruit slices to the side. Other vegetables suitable for serving in this style include different radishes, beets (beetroot), artichokes and carrots.

FIG AND MELON IN PORT WINE

1 small, ripe cantaloupe (rockmelon)
½ cup (4 fl oz/125 ml) good-quality tawny port
4 ripe black figs
freshly ground black pepper
1 tablespoon extra virgin olive oil

Halve cantaloupe lengthwise and remove seeds. Carefully peel each half to ensure a smooth, even surface. Cut each half into 6 equal wedges and gently toss in port. Set aside at room temperature for 30 minutes for port to penetrate fruit, tossing occasionally so all fruit comes into contact with port. To serve, place 3 pieces of cantaloupe on each serving plate; reserve port. Trim stems from figs, cut into quarters and gently roll in port. Place fig pieces on each plate and grind over some fresh pepper. Swirl olive oil in port and drizzle over fruit. Serve immediately.

Serves 4

Note If you include meat in your diet, this dish is excellent with Italian prosciutto crudo ham that has been salt-cured and air-dried. Paper-thin slices are a perfect complement to figs, melon and port. Port wine is fortified with a spirit and some styles (young ruby ports) may be pasteurized, which means they will have been heated.

GREEN AND YELLOW BEANS WITH WALNUT SAUCE

¾ cup (3 oz/90 g) freshly shelled walnuts

1 clove garlic

¼ cup (2 fl oz/60 ml) extra virgin olive oil

1 tablespoon walnut oil, plus extra for drizzling

1 tablespoon lemon juice

sea salt

2 tablespoons cold water

7 oz (200 g) yellow beans, stalks only trimmed

7 oz (200 g) green beans, stalks only trimmed

freshly ground black pepper

½ cup (½ oz/15 g) flat-leaf (Italian) parsley leaves

4 small lemon wedges, to serve

Place ½ cup (2 oz/60 g) walnuts in a blender with garlic, olive oil, walnut oil, lemon juice, a pinch of salt and cold water. Blend until smooth and set aside. Bring a small pan of water to a boil and remove from heat. Add beans and set aside, uncovered, for 3 minutes. Drain and toss with a little walnut oil and a pinch each of salt and pepper. Break remaining walnuts into pieces and toss through beans with parsley leaves. Serve on warmed plates with walnut sauce and lemon wedges. Drizzle walnut oil around the edge of each mound of beans.

Serves 4

Note To avoid placing beans in boiling water, cut them very finely lengthwise and proceed with the recipe. If walnut oil is unavailable, use extra virgin olive oil. Old walnuts can be bitter, so use freshly shelled ones if you can.

MIXED MARINATED OLIVES WITH HERBS AND CELERY

1 cup (6 oz/180 g) giant green olives

1 cup (6 oz/180 g) Kalamata olives

1 cup (6 oz/180 g) small green olives

1 cup (6 oz/180 g) niçoise or dry-cured black olives

4 cloves garlic

½ red bell pepper (capsicum), seeded and finely sliced

2 inner celery stalks with leaves attached, coarsely chopped

1–2 bird's eye chili, seeded and finely sliced

4 fresh or 2 dried bay leaves

2 sprigs oregano or marjoram

3 sprigs thyme

4 sprigs parsley

6 black peppercorns

about 2 cups (16 fl oz/500 ml) extra virgin olive oil

Keeping different types separate, rinse olives in cold water and thoroughly pat dry with paper towels. Mix all olives together in a large bowl. Gently crush each garlic clove with back of a knife so insides are exposed but cloves remain in one piece. Mix through olives along with bell pepper, celery, chili, bay leaves, herbs and peppercorns. Sterilize a large jar by simmering it gently in a large pan of water for 10 minutes, then drain and allow to dry in an oven preheated to 300°F (150°C/Gas 2). Fill with olives while still warm, then add enough olive oil to cover. Seal and set aside at room temperature for a couple of days to allow flavors to develop. To serve, remove olives from oil. As olives are consumed, drain

flavored oil and use it to make dressings, always leaving just enough to cover olives.

Makes 4 cups

Note If you are making smaller quantities to use within a week or so, you can marinate the olives in a ceramic dish in the refrigerator, rather than a sterilized jar. The celery and bell pepper, in addition to imparting flavor and looking attractive, may also be eaten.

SPICED VEGETABLE CRISPS

1 medium parsnip, finely sliced on the diagonal

2 medium tomatoes, finely sliced

1 medium red onion, finely sliced into rings

1 medium beet (beetroot), finely sliced into rounds

1 medium zucchini (courgette), finely sliced into rounds

1–2 tablespoons extra virgin olive oil

1 tablespoon chopped mixed herbs (optional)

1 teaspoon ground red chili

freshly ground black pepper

sea salt

Spread vegetable slices out on a dehydrator sheet or nonstick baking sheet. Mix olive oil, herbs and chili with a pinch of pepper and brush the surface of each piece with oil. Dry out either in a dehydrator or oven set to 110°F (55°C) for 2–6 hours until frilly at the edges and crisp (the time will vary depending on the thickness of the vegetables and the rate at which the moisture evaporates in your oven or dehydrator). Remove from dehydrator or oven, sprinkle with a pinch of salt and cool. To serve, gently mix crisps together and serve as a snack with fresh vegetables or marinated olives.

Serves 2–4

Variation To give crisps a hint of garlic, crush a clove of garlic into olive oil and allow it to infuse for 10 minutes before brushing onto vegetables.

SPICY MIXED NUTS

½ cup (2 oz/60 g) unpeeled almonds

½ cup (2 oz/60 g) macadamias

½ cup (2 oz/60 g) cashews

½ cup (2 oz/60 g) pistachios

½ cup (2 oz/60 g) peanuts

½ cup (2 oz/60 g) hazelnuts

½ cup (2 oz/60 g) Brazil nuts

3 tablespoons pepitas (pumpkin seeds)

2 tablespoons unhulled sesame seeds

½ teaspoon ground turmeric or ground cumin

½ teaspoon cayenne pepper

1 teaspoon sea salt

¼ teaspoon freshly ground back pepper

1 tablespoon extra virgin olive oil

Mix nuts and seeds together in a bowl and set aside. Combine seasonings, then toss through nuts to disperse. Drizzle over oil and toss well to coat nuts and seeds. Spread mix out on a dehydrator sheet or nonstick baking sheet and dry out either in a dehydrator or oven set to 110°F (55°C). The process may take 6–12 hours. Nuts are ready when they are crisp and fragrant. Remove from dehydrator or oven and cool before storing in an airtight container. Serve alone, with drinks or to spice up salads.

Makes about 2½ cups

Variation To give nuts an Asian flavor, omit turmeric or cumin, halve salt, and add ½ teaspoon or unpasteurized soy sauce to mix before drying.

TOMATO-AND-BASIL-STUFFED MUSHROOMS

8 large common white (field) mushrooms

4 cloves garlic, finely chopped

1 tablespoon sherry vinegar

sea salt

freshly ground black pepper

5 tablespoons olive oil

20 sun-dried tomato quarters, finely chopped

½ cup (2 oz/60 g) pine nuts

½ cup (½ oz/15 g) finely chopped flat-leaf (Italian) parsley

½ cup (½ oz/15 g) finely chopped basil

Remove stems from mushrooms and discard. Gently wipe surface of each mushroom with a soft cloth to remove any dirt. Peel mushrooms with your fingers by pulling flesh from under each hood up and over the surface of each mushroom. Continue working your way around until mushroom is peeled (this is very quick once you get the hang of it). Repeat with remaining mushrooms. Finely chop skins and set aside. Combine 2 cloves garlic, sherry vinegar, a pinch each of salt and pepper, and 3 tablespoons olive oil, then marinate mushrooms by brushing top and bottom with mixture. Set aside at room temperature.

To make the filling, place chopped mushroom skins in a bowl with remaining garlic and olive oil, tomato, pine nuts, parsley and basil. Stir to combine and season to taste with salt and pepper. Spread mushrooms out on a dehydrator sheet or nonstick baking sheet. Spoon equal amounts of filling into each mushroom. Dry out either in a dehydrator or oven set to 110°F (55°C) for 2–4 hours until softened. Remove from dehydrator or oven and serve on warmed plates.

Serves 4

Note To dry your own tomatoes, see page 103.

VEGETABLE CRUDITÉS WITH HUMMUS

1 cup (8 oz/250 g) chickpeas (garbanzo beans)

1–2 tablespoons raw tahini

2 cloves garlic, crushed

2 tablespoons lemon juice

2 tablespoons water

¼ teaspoon chili powder

1 teaspoon ground cumin

⅓ cup (3 fl oz/90 ml) extra virgin olive oil

sea salt

freshly ground black pepper

2 lemon wedges

¼ cup (1 oz/30 g) small black olives

2–4 cups trimmed fresh vegetables, left whole or cut into strips or sticks, such as carrot, snow peas, sugar snaps, young green beans, bell pepper (capsicum), Belgian endive leaves, broccoli florets, zucchini (courgette), cucumber, celery, radish, asparagus, tomato wedges

To make chickpea sprouts follow directions on page 21.

In a food processor, place chickpea sprouts, tahini, garlic, lemon juice, water, spices and olive oil and process until very smooth. Add a little more water if mixture looks too thick. Add salt and pepper to taste, then transfer to a serving bowl in center of a platter of prepared vegetables for dipping.

Makes about 2 cups; serves 4–8

Variation To make a meal of dips and vegetables, serve both Black Olive Tapenade (see page 96) and Dried Tomato Paste dip (see page 98) alongside hummus and ensure you have a good range of dipping vegetables.

VINE LEAVES STUFFED WITH PINE NUTS, CURRANTS AND SWISS CHARD (DOLMAS)

12 Swiss chard (silverbeet) leaves, white stems
    removed, chopped
1 shallot (French shallot), sliced
2 cloves garlic, crushed
4 teaspoons lemon juice
1 cup (4 oz/125 g) pine nuts, soaked overnight in
    water and drained
½ cup (2 oz/60 g) dried currants, soaked in water
    1 hour and drained
1 cup (3 oz/90 g) bean sprouts
⅓ cup (⅓ oz/10 g) chopped mint
¼ cup (2 fl oz/60 ml) extra virgin olive oil,
    plus 2–3 tablespoons
sea salt
freshly ground black pepper
12 large grape (vine) leaves, preserved in brine

In a food processor, place Swiss chard, shallot, garlic, lemon juice, pine nuts, currants, bean sprouts and mint, then pulse a few times. Pour in ¼ cup olive oil and process until well combined but not smooth, it should still have plenty of texture. Season to taste with salt and pepper and set aside. Carefully rinse grape (vine) leaves in cold water and pat dry with paper towels. Place 1 leaf on a work surface with the inside of the leaf facing up. Brush leaf with olive oil and place about 2 tablespoons filling in center in a rectangular shape. Fold base of leaf up over filling and brush with oil. Fold side edges in and brush, then roll up firmly but gently into the shape of a dolma. Brush any remaining exposed leaf surface with olive oil and set aside on a tray. Repeat with remaining leaves and filling, then refrigerate for a few hours, or until firm. When ready to serve, gently slice in half on diagonal and serve with cut surface facing up.

Makes 12

ZUCCHINI STRIPS WITH CHARMOULA

1 cup (1 oz/30 g) coarsely chopped cilantro
   (fresh coriander)
1 cup (1 oz/30 g) coarsely chopped flat-leaf
   (Italian) parsley
4 cloves garlic, crushed
1 tablespoon ground cumin
½ teaspoon ground red chili
2 tablespoons lemon juice
½ cup (4 fl oz/125 ml) extra virgin olive oil
sea salt
freshly ground black pepper
6 large zucchini (courgettes)

To make charmoula, mix together cilantro, parsley, garlic, cumin, chili and lemon juice, then stir in olive oil. Season to taste with salt and pepper (the mix will be quite pungent) and set aside. Trim zucchini and slice lengthwise on a Japanese vegetable slicer or mandoline. The slices should be very thin. Curl and fold zucchini slices into attractive shapes so they do not sit flat, and arrange on serving plates. Spoon over charmoula and serve.

Serves 4–6

Note Charmoula is a Moroccan marinade and seasoning most commonly used on fish and shellfish. It is intensely pungent, and can be used over any vegetables that are good to eat raw. For an extra lemony boost, try adding a small amount of chopped Preserved Lemon (see page 102).

Soups

AJO BLANCO
(SPANISH CHILLED ALMOND AND GRAPE SOUP)

1 cup (4 oz/125 g) unpeeled almonds, soaked
    overnight in cold water and peeled
1¾ cups (14 fl oz/440 ml) almond milk (see page 27)
2 cloves garlic, crushed
2 cups (16 fl oz/500 ml) water
2 tablespoons sherry vinegar
⅓ cup (3 fl oz/90 ml) extra virgin olive oil,
    plus extra to serve
sea salt
freshly ground white pepper
40–50 seedless white grapes
2 tablespoons snipped chives

Blend almonds and almond milk just until well combined, then cover and refrigerate overnight. Next day, pour almonds and milk into a blender, add garlic and water and blend until completely smooth. Add sherry vinegar and olive oil, season to taste with salt and pepper and blend again. Cover and chill completely. Meanwhile, peel each grape (the effort will be worth it) and cut in half lengthwise. To serve, stir soup, then pour into chilled serving bowls. Divide grapes and chives among the bowls, drizzle a little olive oil on the surface and serve.

Serves 4

Note A high-speed blender will give a silky smooth soup, but if the almonds have not been completely broken down, the soup may be strained after adding the garlic and water. The success and authenticity of this dish relies on good-quality sherry vinegar, so don't be tempted to skimp or substitute.

ARUGULA, WALNUT AND JERUSALEM ARTICHOKE SOUP

1 shallot (French shallot), finely sliced

1 lemon, cut in half crosswise

2 cups (9 oz/270 g) Jerusalem artichokes

1 clove garlic, crushed

2 small celery stalks, chopped

3 cups (3 oz/90 g) chopped arugula (rocket)

½ cup (2 oz/60 g) walnuts

¼ cup (¼ oz/7 g) chopped parsley

2 tablespoons sherry vinegar or lemon juice

sea salt

freshly ground black pepper

¼ cup (2 fl oz/60 ml) extra virgin olive oil

2 cups (16 fl oz/500 ml) water

1–2 tablespoons walnut oil (optional)

2 tablespoons snipped chives

Soften shallot in a dehydrator or oven set to 110°F (55°C) for 1 hour (or soak in water for 30 minutes) to reduce its pungency. Meanwhile, squeeze lemon into a bowl of water and add squeezed lemon halves. Peel artichokes and immediately place each one into acidulated water to prevent oxidization. When shallot is ready, place in a blender with garlic, celery, arugula, walnuts, parsley, vinegar and a pinch each of salt and pepper. Add olive oil and half the water and blend until smooth. Coarsely chop artichokes and add to the mix, blending until very smooth. Add remaining water and check seasoning. Add a little more water if soup is too thick. Serve in warmed soup bowls with a splash of walnut oil and a sprinkle of chives on top.

Serves 4

Variation Young spinach leaves can be substituted for arugula, and walnuts can be replaced with hazelnuts. Wild arugula is too strong a flavor for this dish, so choose a milder large-leaf variety.

AVOCADO AND CORN SOUP WITH CHILI AND CILANTRO

3 large, ripe avocados, pits and skins removed

3 tablespoons lemon juice

1 English (hothouse) or 2 Lebanese cucumbers, peeled and coarsely chopped

2 ripe tomatoes, peeled, seeded and chopped

2 ears (cobs) of corn

¼ cup (¼ oz/7 g) chopped flat-leaf (Italian) parsley leaves

2 teaspoons finely chopped cilantro (fresh coriander) root

1 bird's eye chili, seeded and finely sliced

2 cups (16 fl oz/500 ml) water

sea salt

freshly ground white pepper

½ small red bell pepper (capsicum), seeded

½ teaspoon extra virgin olive oil

½ cup (½ oz/15 g) cilantro (fresh coriander) sprigs

In a blender, place avocado flesh, lemon juice, cucumber and tomato and puree until smooth. Cut the corn ears in half through center, then grate each piece in turn until kernels are reduced to a vibrant yellow pulp. Add to avocado mixture along with parsley, cilantro root, chili and water. Blend until smooth, then season to taste with salt and pepper. Add a little more water if you prefer a thinner soup. Cut bell pepper in half, then cut each in half through its thickness to give 4 very thin rectangles of flesh. Cut each into paper-thin strips, then toss together with olive oil and cilantro sprigs. Divide soup among serving bowls and garnish with pepper and cilantro.

Serves 4

Variation All these soup ingredients could be cut into bite-size pieces, tossed together and served as a salad.

CHILLED CUCUMBER SOUP WITH RED RADISHES

3 English (hothouse) or 6 Lebanese cucumbers,
    peeled and coarsely chopped
1 cup (3 oz/90 g) finely sliced scallion
    (shallot/spring onion)
¼ cup (2 fl oz/60 ml) water
4½ teaspoons lemon juice
sea salt
freshly ground white pepper
green tops from 2 scallions (shallots/spring onions)
4 small red radishes
½ teaspoon extra virgin olive oil
4–8 chervil sprigs (optional)

In a blender, place cucumber, finely sliced scallion, water and 4 teaspoons lemon juice and blend until very smooth. Season to taste with salt and pepper. Cover and chill completely. Make scallion curls by slicing 4-inch (10-cm) lengths of the dark green part into very thin strips. Plunge into iced water for about 10 minutes. Meanwhile, finely slice radishes into rounds using a Japanese vegetable slicer or mandoline on its finest setting. Drain scallion curls and toss together with radish slices, olive oil, chervil and a pinch each of salt and pepper. To serve, stir cucumber soup, pour into chilled bowls and top with garnish.

Serves 2–4

Variation If chervil is unavailable, either dill or chives could be used. To vary the garnish and further chill the soup, set chervil or dill sprigs in ice blocks and add to soup on serving.

CREAMED CAULIFLOWER SOUP

1 head (about 2 lb/1 kg before trimming)
   cauliflower, cut into florets
¼ cup (2 fl oz/60 ml) lemon juice
2 teaspoons ground cumin
½ cup (4 fl oz/125 ml) extra virgin olive oil
2 cups (16 fl oz/500 ml) water
sea salt
freshly ground pepper
2 tablespoons finely chopped parsley
2 tablespoons finely chopped cilantro
   (fresh coriander)

In a high-speed blender, place cauliflower florets, lemon juice, cumin, olive oil and water and blend until very smooth. Season to taste with salt and pepper, then sieve, carefully pressing as much liquid as possible from pulp. Check seasoning, then pour soup into warmed serving bowls and scatter with parsley and cilantro.

Serves 4

Note The texture of this soup is so smooth and the flavor so creamy, it's hard to believe it is dairy free.

TOMATO AND MINT "GAZPACHO"

3 lb (1.5 kg) ripe tomatoes, cored and coarsely
   chopped
1 English (hothouse) or 2 Lebanese cucumbers,
   coarsely chopped
2 red bell peppers (capsicum), seeded and coarsely
   chopped
3 cloves garlic, crushed
⅔ cup (2 oz/60 g) almond meal (see note page 92)
2 cups (16 fl oz/500 ml) water
1 tablespoon sea salt
1½ teaspoons freshly ground black pepper
½ cup (½ oz/15 g) mint leaves, finely chopped
⅓ cup (3 fl oz/90 ml) sherry vinegar
⅔ cup (5 fl oz/150 ml) extra virgin olive oil
inner celery stalks, leaves attached

Stir together all ingredients except celery in a large, nonreactive bowl and cover tightly. Chill for at least 2 hours to allow flavors to develop. Puree soup in a blender just until it is half blended. There should not be large chunks, but it should not be smooth and well combined either. Check seasoning, then pour into serving cups or glasses and serve with celery sticks.

Serves 6–8

Note As with Ajo Blanco (see page 48), the success of this soup depends on a good-quality sherry vinegar.

Salads and vegetables

ARTICHOKE, CELERY AND PINE NUT SALAD WITH THYME AND LEMON DRESSING

3 tablespoons lemon juice

1 teaspoon lemon zest

½ cup (3½ oz/110 g) finely diced peeled tomato

2 teaspoons fresh lemon thyme or thyme leaves

sea salt

freshly ground black pepper

¾ cup (6 fl oz/180 ml) extra virgin olive oil

1 lemon, cut in half crosswise

6 medium artichokes

2 inner celery stalks with leaves attached, finely sliced

¼ cup (1 oz/30 g) pine nuts

2 cups (2 oz/60 g) baby curly endive

¼ cup (¼ oz/7 g) chervil sprigs (optional)

To make dressing, stir together lemon juice and zest, tomato, thyme, pinch each salt and pepper, then whisk in all but 2 tablespoons olive oil. Check seasoning and set aside.

Squeeze lemon juice into a bowl of cold water, then add lemon halves as well. To prepare artichokes one at a time, trim stalks so that 1 inch (2.5 cm) remains at the base, then remove and discard outer leaves. As center of the artichoke is revealed, begin tearing each leaf downward so that the tender heart and stalk remain. Nibble on the base of a leaf to see whether it's tender; if not, continue removing leaves. Trim outer skin of the base, then trim thistles off top. Cut artichoke heart lengthwise to reveal the thistle-like choke and remove every scrap of it with a small spoon or knife. Place halves into acidulated water and repeat with remaining artichokes. When they are all done, cut each half lengthwise into paper-thin slices and toss immediately into dressing to prevent oxidation. Add celery, pine nuts and endive and toss well. Transfer salad to serving plates and drizzle remaining olive oil around edge of each plate. Scatter with chervil if using.

Serves 4–6

BABY LEEKS WITH GREEN OLIVE AND CAPER TAPENADE

1 cup (6 oz/180 g) pitted green olives

1 tablespoon nonpareil (baby) capers, rinsed and patted dry

2 cloves garlic

½ cup (½ oz/15 g) chopped parsley

1 tablespoon thyme leaves

1 teaspoon lemon zest

½ cup (4 fl oz/125 ml) extra virgin olive oil

sea salt

freshly ground black pepper

12–16 baby leeks

In a food processor, place olives, capers, garlic, parsley, thyme and lemon zest and pulse until a paste begins to form. Add all but 2 tablespoons olive oil and process to combine. If you prefer a smooth tapenade, continue processing until your preferred consistency is achieved. Season to taste with salt and pepper, then cover and set aside. Remove coarse outer leaves from leeks and discard. Trim leek tops to ¾ inch (2 cm) above the white part and discard. Trim leek bases to remove any root or dirt and leave core so the leek stays together. Cut each leek lengthwise from top to ¼ inch (0.5 cm) from base, so leek is in two parts but still joined together. Bring a pan of water to a boil, remove from heat, immerse leeks in water for 2 minutes and drain; or steam over a pan of boiling water for 2 minutes. Season leeks with salt and pepper and a little reserved olive oil. Divide leeks among warmed serving plates, spoon tapenade on top and drizzle with remaining oil. Serve immediately.

Serves 4

Note If you prefer not to blanch or steam leeks, they can be tossed in a little olive oil and water and softened in a dehydrator or oven set to 110°F (55°C) for 1–2 hours.

BEET AND CARROT SALAD WITH WALNUTS

2 tablespoons apple cider vinegar

sea salt

freshly ground black pepper

¼ cup (2 fl oz/60 ml) extra virgin olive oil

3 cups (10 oz/300 g) grated beet (beetroot)

3 cups (10 oz/300 g) grated carrot

½ cup (2 oz/60 g) coarsely chopped walnuts

1 cup (1 oz/30 g) torn flat-leaf (Italian) parsley
   leaves

½ cup (½ oz/15 g) snipped chives

In a bowl, place vinegar, a pinch each of salt and pepper, and olive oil and whisk to combine with a fork. Add grated beet and carrot and toss thoroughly, then set aside at room temperature for about 10 minutes, tossing occasionally, so carrot picks up the beet's color and dressing permeates. Add walnuts and parsley, toss again and serve in mounds on serving plates. Sprinkle with chives and serve.

Serves 4

Variation To increase the energy of the salad, include chunks of ripe avocado or a sprinkling of dried vine fruits such as currants or raisins. For a change, walnuts can be replaced with an equal amount of sunflower seeds.

BLACK OLIVE, FIG, AND ARUGULA SALAD

1 tablespoon aged balsamic vinegar

sea salt

freshly ground black pepper

3 tablespoons extra virgin olive oil

4–6 ripe black or green figs

6½ oz (200 g) arugula (rocket) or wild arugula

½ cup (3 oz/90 g) small black olives such as niçoise

Place vinegar in a bowl with a pinch each of salt and pepper, then whisk in olive oil. Check seasoning. Trim fig stems, cut into quarters and gently fold through dressing. Add arugula and olives and turn to coat with dressing. Transfer to serving plates and eat at once.

Serves 4

Variation To intensify the fig flavor of this salad, slice 2 ripe figs very thinly and spread out on a dehydrator sheet or nonstick baking sheet. Brush the surface of each piece lightly with a little olive oil and sprinkle with a tiny amount of black pepper. Dry out either in a dehydrator or oven set to 110°F (55°C) for 2–4 hours until curled at the edges and crisp. Remove from dehydrator or oven and cool. Place fig crisps on salad. If figs are unavailable, 2 ripe pears can be substituted.

BOK CHOY WITH ASIAN MUSHROOMS MARINATED IN GINGER SOY DRESSING

For the dressing

1 tablespoon finely grated fresh ginger

1 clove garlic, crushed

2 tablespoons unpasteurized soy sauce (nama shoyu)

1 tablespoon lime juice

¼ cup (2 fl oz/60 ml) cold-pressed sesame oil

freshly ground black pepper

10 oz (300 g) mixed fresh Asian mushrooms
   such as shiitake, oyster and enokitake

2 bunches bok choy, halved lengthwise

¼ cup (¼ oz/7 g) cilantro (fresh coriander) leaves

Mix together ginger, garlic, soy sauce, lime juice and sesame oil and season with a pinch of pepper. Prepare mushrooms by wiping with a damp cloth if there are any dirt spots. Remove and discard shiitake mushroom stems. Slice shiitake thinly and toss in dressing. Add whole oyster mushrooms, or cut in half if large. Gently break enokitake into small bundles and gently fold through dressing with other mushrooms. Set aside to marinate for up to 1 hour. When mushrooms are done, bring a pan of water to a boil, remove from heat, immerse bok choy into water for 1 minute and drain well, or steam over a pan of boiling water for 1 minute. Toss bok choy through mushrooms and dressing. Check seasoning and garnish with cilantro.

Serves 4

Note If you prefer not to blanch or steam bok choy, shred it finely, then add to marinated mushrooms and toss together. Marinate altogether for a further 30 minutes before serving.

BROCCOLINI WITH FERMENTED BLACK BEANS

2 tablespoons fermented black beans
2 teaspoons sherry vinegar
1 shallot (French shallot), finely sliced
1 bird's eye chili, seeded and finely chopped
2 bunches broccolini (see note) or 1 head broccoli
2 tablespoons extra virgin olive oil
freshly ground black pepper
1 tablespoon chopped garlic chives

Rinse black beans in cold water as many as 10 or 20 times to reduce saltiness. Use fresh water each time you rinse. Drain well and set aside. In a bowl, place sherry vinegar, shallot and chili and whisk with a fork to combine. Add black beans and mash into remaining ingredients with back of the fork. Set aside to steep. Trim broccolini (do not peel, as its stalks are entirely tender). If using broccoli, peel coarse skin away by pulling rather than cutting. (It's just like peeling a fig. You catch a broken piece of skin with edge of a knife then pull a strip away; it follows natural contours.) Leaving as much stalk attached as possible, cut broccolini into evenly sized florets with long strips of stalk. Bring a small pan of water to a boil, remove from heat and immerse broccolini florets for 2–3 minutes. Meanwhile, whisk 1 1/2 tablespoons olive oil into black bean mixture and season with pepper to taste. Drain broccolini, toss well with remaining olive oil, and then toss through dressing. Sprinkle with garlic chives and serve on warmed plates.

Serves 2

Note Broccolini is a vegetable developed to mimic the tender green shoots of broccoli just as it goes to seed. Fermented black (soy) beans, a staple ingredient in Chinese cooking, are sold either in cans or jars of salty brine, or packed in salt crystals. Either type is fine, as long as the beans are well rinsed to the stage that the complex fermented bean flavor, rather than just salt, can be tasted. They may also be labeled "preserved black beans."

Variation Ginger, garlic and scallions also work well with black beans.

CARROT STICK SALAD WITH CILANTRO AND CHILI

For the dressing
1 clove garlic, crushed
1 teaspoon coarsely crushed cumin seeds
1 bird's eye chili, seeded and finely sliced
2 tablespoons lemon juice
sea salt
freshly ground black pepper
2 tablespoons extra virgin olive oil

3–4 (14 oz/400g) carrots, peeled and cut into
    batons 2 inches (5 cm) long and ¼ inch (0.5 cm)
    square
¼ cup (¼ oz/7 g) chopped cilantro (fresh
    coriander)
2 oz (60 g) pea shoots or mustard cress
½ tablespoon extra virgin olive oil

To make dressing: In a bowl, place garlic, cumin, chili and lemon juice, season with salt and pepper and whisk in olive oil. Check seasoning and set aside.

Bring a pan of water to a boil, remove from heat and immerse carrots in water. Drain immediately and toss in dressing. Stir through cilantro. Dress pea shoots with olive oil and season. Serve carrots on a bed of pea shoots.

Note If you prefer not to plunge carrots into hot water, simply grate them instead and proceed with the recipe.

Serves 2–4

CELERY AND RED APPLE SALAD WITH WALNUTS AND "MAYONNAISE"

For the dressing

½ cup (2 oz/60 g) macadamia or pine nuts, soaked
    in water overnight
1 clove garlic, crushed
1 tablespoon chopped flat-leaf (Italian) parsley
2 tablespoons lemon juice
⅓ cup (3 fl oz/90 ml) water
3 tablespoons extra virgin olive oil
sea salt
freshly ground black pepper

2 crisp red apples, unpeeled
4 celery stalks with leaves attached, finely sliced on
    the diagonal
½ cup (2 oz/60 g) walnut pieces
4 lettuce leaf cups (optional)
1 tablespoon extra virgin olive oil

To make dressing: Drain nuts, discard soaking water and blend to a smooth paste with garlic, parsley, lemon juice and water. Add olive oil and blend until smooth and creamy. Season to taste with salt and pepper and set aside.

Cut apples into quarters, remove cores and cut into chunks. Place in a large bowl with celery, add dressing and toss together. Stir well, then add walnuts. Serve in bowls or lettuce cups if using and drizzle with olive oil.

Note If you include classic raw egg mayonnaise in your diet, you could substitute 1 cup (8 fl oz/250 ml) of it for the dressing above. This nut version makes about 1 cup (8 fl oz/250 ml) of dressing and can be used on other fresh vegetable and fruit salads. Using a high-speed blender to make it will give a smoother, more mayonnaise-like result.

Serves 4

GREEN APPLE AND RADICCHIO SALAD WITH ALMOND DRESSING

For the dressing

⅓ cup (1½ oz/45 g) unpeeled almonds, soaked in
  water overnight and peeled

2 inner celery stalks with leaves attached, coarsely
  chopped

1 clove garlic

¼ cup (2 fl oz/60 ml) lemon juice

½ cup (½ oz/15 g) flat-leaf (Italian) parsley leaves

sea salt

freshly ground pepper

3 green apples, unpeeled

2 heads radicchio, outer leaves discarded, cut into
  julienne

⅓ cup (2 oz/60 g) raisins

2 tablespoons extra virgin olive oil

Blend almonds, celery, garlic, lemon juice and half the parsley until smooth. Season to taste with salt and pepper and set aside.

Cut each apple into fine julienne strips by cutting thin slices from one side of the apple, then the other, then the 2 remaining slim pieces until you are left with just the core, stacking as you go. Then cut slices into strips. Toss apple and dressing together as quickly as possible to prevent oxidation, then toss through radicchio and raisins to combine. Transfer salad to serving plates, slice remaining parsley into strips and scatter on top. Drizzle with olive oil and serve.

Serves 4

JERUSALEM ARTICHOKE AND SPINACH SALAD WITH HAZELNUT DRESSING

½ shallot (French shallot), finely sliced

2 tablespoons lemon juice, plus 1 lemon, cut in half crosswise

2 tablespoons extra virgin olive oil

2 tablespoons hazelnut oil or extra virgin olive oil

sea salt

freshly ground black pepper

4 oz (125 g) oyster mushrooms (optional)

2 cups (9 oz/270 g) Jerusalem artichokes

3 cups (3 oz/90 g) baby spinach (English spinach) leaves

¼ cup (1½ oz/45 g) coarsely chopped hazelnuts

In a large bowl, mix together shallot, lemon juice and olive oil with half the hazelnut oil. Season with salt and pepper. Pour half the dressing into a smaller bowl and toss with oyster mushrooms. Set aside for 10 minutes so mushrooms pick up the flavor of the dressing and begin to soften. Meanwhile, squeeze lemon into a bowl of water and add the squeezed lemon halves. Peel Jerusalem artichokes and immediately place each one into acidulated water to prevent oxidization. One by one, very finely slice artichokes using a Japanese vegetable slicer or mandoline on its finest setting. As each artichoke is sliced, toss in plain dressing. Continue until all artichokes are sliced. Add dressed mushrooms to artichokes, then toss through spinach leaves and hazelnuts. Transfer to serving plates and drizzle remaining hazelnut oil around each salad.

Serves 4

Note Good-quality nut oils have a flavor and aroma that gives an inimitable lift to salads such as this. They are often used simply for finishing a dish rather than as a major component, which means a little will go a long way. Buy small amounts of different nut oils from a reputable store, check the expiry date, and store in the refrigerator in a glass jar or metal tin to maintain freshness.

MACERATED LEMON AND TOMATO SALAD

1 lb (500 g) multicolored small tomatoes such as red or ripe green cherry, yellow tear drop and purple heritage varieties, rinsed and patted dry
sea salt
freshly ground black pepper
½ teaspoon lemon zest
1 shallot (French shallot), finely sliced
1 teaspoon lemon thyme or thyme leaves
¼ cup (2 fl oz/60 ml) extra virgin olive oil
2 oz (60 g) pea shoots (optional)
4 small lemon wedges

Cut tomatoes in half lengthwise and season with salt and pepper. Toss gently together with lemon zest, shallot, thyme and olive oil. Cover and set aside at room temperature for 20 minutes for the flavors to develop. Check seasoning and serve as is or combine with pea shoots. Garnish with lemon wedges.

Serves 2–3

Variation Omit lemon zest and replace with ½ cup (½ oz/15 g) fresh basil leaves. To increase the energy of the salad, both versions are delicious with chunks of avocado added just before serving. For an even more substantial version, add freshly sprouted chickpeas (garbanzo beans, see page 21).

ORANGE, RED ONION AND OLIVE SALAD

4 large oranges, skin and pith removed
½ red onion, finely sliced into half-moons
2 tablespoons orange juice
sea salt
freshly ground black pepper
¼ cup (2 fl oz/60 ml) extra virgin olive oil
½ cup (3 oz/90 g) small black olives such as niçoise
4 sprigs marjoram, leaves removed

Thinly slice oranges and spread each sliced orange in an overlapping circle on 4 serving plates. Rinse red onion in cold water to remove some of its pungency, then drain and pat dry with paper towels. In a small bowl, mix together onion, orange juice, salt and pepper to taste, and olive oil. Add olives. Make a mound of salad in the center of each orange circle and drizzle dressing over the orange slices as you go. Scatter marjoram leaves on top and serve immediately.

Serves 4

Variation If you find the flavor of raw onion too pungent, either soak it in cold water for 30 minutes before draining and patting dry, or replace onion with ½ cup (1½ oz/45 g) finely sliced scallion (shallot/spring onion). For an extra cooling boost, add chunks of peeled cucumber to the onion dressing.

PEAR, WALNUT AND BITTER GREENS SALAD

2 firm, ripe pears such as Beurre Bosc, unpeeled
¼ cup (2 fl oz/60 ml) extra virgin olive oil
freshly ground black pepper
1 tablespoon smooth or mild mustard, such as Dijon
1 teaspoon white wine or sherry vinegar
sea salt
3 Asian pears (nashi), unpeeled
4 cups (4 oz/125 g) mixed bitter salad leaves such
    as Belgian endive, radicchio and baby curly
    endive
½ cup (2 oz/60 g) coarsely chopped walnuts
½ cup (½ oz/15 g) chervil sprigs (optional)

Wash and dry pears, then slice as thinly as possible using a Japanese vegetable slicer or mandoline. Slice each pear with blossom end facing base of slicer and stem facing top. Slice down to core, then turn pear over and slice other side down to core. Ideally each slice will be fringed with skin. Spread pear slices out on a dehydrator sheet or nonstick baking sheet. Brush slices lightly with 1 tablespoon olive oil and sprinkle with a tiny amount of pepper. Dry out either in a dehydrator or oven set to 110°F (55°C) for 2–4 hours until frilly at the edges and crisp. Remove from dehydrator or oven and cool. In a bowl, place mustard and vinegar and whisk in remaining olive oil. Season to taste with salt and pepper. Cut Asian pears into quarters, remove cores, then cut into even-sized chunks. Toss through dressing to coat. Choose small salad leaves or slice larger ones finely and toss with Asian pears. Add walnuts then transfer to serving plates and garnish with chervil if using. Place a pile of dried pear crisps on top of each salad.

Serves 4

Variation Try this salad with different combinations of bitter salad leaves such as all-green arugula (rocket), watercress and mustard cress or try pungent edible flowers and leaves, such as nasturtium. You can make the same salad using apples; simply slice and dry 2 cooking apples in place of the regular pears, and use 3 fresh green apples in place of the Asian pears.

PINK GRAPEFRUIT, FENNEL AND RED ONION SALAD

2 pink grapefruits

1 tablespoon fennel seeds, crushed

2 tablespoons smooth or mild mustard, such as Dijon

1 clove garlic, crushed

⅓ cup (3 fl oz/90 ml) extra virgin olive oil

2 medium bulbs (1¼ lb/625 g) fennel with fronds

sea salt

freshly ground black pepper

½ medium red onion, sliced crosswise paper-thin

2 cups (2 oz/60 g) watercress sprigs

Remove skin and pith from grapefruits, closely following shape of the fruit. Cut each grapefruit into segments and set aside. Squeeze juice from membrane that remains and place juice in a nonreactive bowl. Add crushed fennel seeds, mustard and garlic and stir to combine. Gradually whisk in all but 1 tablespoon oil to make a thick dressing. Trim fronds from fennel and finely chop enough to yield 2 tablespoons. Stir through dressing and season to taste. Set aside. Cut fennel bulb in half and remove core. Using a sharp knife, cut lengthwise into paper-thin slices. Toss fennel, onion and grapefruit segments through dressing. Serve on a bed of watercress in shallow bowls and drizzle with reserved olive oil.

Serves 4–6

Note Mustard is usually made by simply mixing ground mustard seed with vinegar. However, as it is sometimes heated during processing, you may wish to check the origins of your preferred brand.

Variation If pink grapefruit is unavailable, use yellow grapefruit. Or, for a sweeter salad, use segments or slices of 3 juicy oranges.

PISTACHIO, CELERY AND CUCUMBER SALAD WITH DATES

⅓ cup (1½ oz/45 g) pistachios, coarsely chopped
sea salt
freshly ground black pepper
⅓ cup (3 fl oz/90 ml) extra virgin olive oil
¼ cup (2 fl oz/60 ml) orange juice
2 tablespoons lemon juice
½ red onion, finely sliced into half-moons
4 large celery stalks, finely sliced on the diagonal
2 English (hothouse) cucumbers, peeled and cut
   into chunks
8 dates, pitted and chopped
¼ cup (¼ oz/7 g) snipped chives

Mix pistachios with a little salt and pepper and ¼ teaspoon olive oil, then spread out on a dehydrator sheet or nonstick baking sheet and dry out either in a dehydrator or oven set to 110°F (55°C) for 1–2 hours until fragrant. Remove from dehydrator or oven, cool, then coarsely chop. In a large bowl, mix orange and lemon juices with remaining olive oil and season to taste with salt and pepper. Rinse onions under cold water, drain, then pat dry (see note on pungency page 72, Orange and Red Onion Salad). Add to dressing along with celery, cucumber and dates. Transfer salad to serving plates, sprinkle with chives and serve immediately.

Serves 4–6

Variation For a lighter version, replace dates with 12–14 seedless red grapes, halved. To enrich the dressing, whisk 2–3 tablespoons oat or seed yogurt (see page 24) into the dressing before adding the other ingredients.

RADISH, KOHLRABI AND DAIKON SALAD

3 small kohlrabi, leaves attached
12 red radishes, leaves trimmed
½ medium daikon, peeled
¼ cup (2 fl oz/60 ml) lemon juice
¼ cup (2 fl oz/60 ml) extra virgin olive oil
sea salt
freshly ground black pepper
¼ cup (¼ oz/7 g) snipped chives
¼ cup (¼ oz/7 g) chervil sprigs

Remove small inner leaves from kohlrabi and set aside. Cut off and discard tough outer leaves (test them by taking a bite). Trim top and base of each kohlrabi as well as leaf roots. Peel kohlrabi only if they are not organic or skin looks tough and blemished. Thinly slice, using a Japanese vegetable slicer or mandoline, directly into a large salad bowl. Holding the stalk of a red radish, carefully slice each one to same thickness as kohlrabi. Slice daikon into rounds. Toss all radishes together with small kohlrabi leaves and set aside. In a small bowl, mix together lemon juice, olive oil and a pinch each of salt and pepper. Toss thoroughly through the radishes, then add chives and chervil. Serve immediately.

Serves 4

Note If you do not have access to a vegetable slicer, coarsely grate the kohlrabi and radishes either by hand or using the grater attachment on a food processor. If you cannot find the kohlrabi as well as both daikon and red radishes, you can use just one or two of the vegetables. Radishes are great for cooling down on a hot day.

RED AND GREEN CABBAGE AND KALE COLESLAW

½ cup (2 oz/60 g) pine nuts

½ cup (2 oz/60 g) macadamia nuts

1 clove garlic, crushed

1 small inner celery stalk, chopped

¼ cup (2 fl oz/60 ml) lemon juice

¼ cup (2 fl oz/60 ml) water

sea salt

freshly ground black pepper

½ cup (4 fl oz/125 ml) extra virgin olive oil

2⅔ cups (8 oz/250 g) very finely shredded Savoy
cabbage

2 cups (6 oz/180 g) very finely shredded red
cabbage

1 cup (3 oz/90 g) very finely shredded kale

4 medium carrots, coarsely grated

½ cup (½ oz/15 g) chopped fresh herbs

In a blender, place nuts, garlic, celery, lemon juice
and water with a pinch each of salt and pepper. Add
half the oil and blend until very smooth. Check
seasoning. Place shredded cabbage and kale in a large
bowl and mix together with carrot, then add dressing
and stir well for 2 minutes to ensure vegetables are
well coated. Cover and set aside for 1 hour or so,
tossing occasionally, until cabbage begins to soften
slightly. When ready to serve, add remaining olive oil
along with herbs, check seasoning and serve in a
large bowl or individual mounds.

Serves 4–8

Variation For an extra flavor dimension, add
1 tablespoon rinsed nonpareil (baby) capers to the
vegetables. If you include raw eggs in your diet, you
could omit the nut dressing above and replace it with
1 cup (8 fl oz/250 ml) or so of freshly made classic
raw egg mayonnaise.

RAINBOW BELL PEPPER SALAD WITH CAPERS AND PRESERVED LEMON

1½ tablespoons red wine vinegar

2 shallots (French shallots), finely sliced

2 cloves garlic, crushed

½ cup (3½ oz/110 g) peeled, seeded and diced
   tomato

2 tablespoons nonpareil (baby) capers, rinsed and
   chopped

¼ teaspoon cayenne pepper

1 tablespoon chopped Preserved Lemon (see note)

⅓ cup (3 fl oz/90 ml) extra virgin olive oil

sea salt

freshly ground black pepper

2 yellow or orange bell peppers (capsicum), seeded
   and very finely sliced lengthwise

2 red bell peppers (capsicum), seeded and very
   finely sliced lengthwise

1 green bell pepper (capsicum), seeded and very
   finely sliced lengthwise

⅓ cup (⅓ oz/10 g) finely sliced flat-leaf (Italian)
   parsley leaves

In a large bowl, stir together vinegar, shallot, garlic, tomato, capers, cayenne and preserved lemon. Whisk in olive oil and season to taste with salt and pepper. Toss through finely sliced bell pepper, cover and set aside for 20 minutes or so, tossing occasionally. After this time bell pepper will have begun to soften slightly and juices will mingle. Check seasoning, add parsley leaves, and transfer to serving plates.

Serves 4–6

Note Preserved Lemons are simple to make (see page 102), and are also widely available at Middle Eastern stores and delicatessens. They have an inimitable delicate lemon flavor that is perfectly matched with capers.

SPINACH LEAF, ORANGE AND AVOCADO SALAD WITH CHICKPEA SPROUTS

¾ cup (6 oz/180 g) chickpeas (garbanzo beans)
  or 1⅓ cups (4 oz/120 g) chickpea sprouts

2 cloves garlic, crushed

1½ tablespoons lemon juice

1½ tablespoons orange juice

2 teaspoons ground cumin

pinch cayenne pepper

¼ cup (2 fl oz/60 ml) extra virgin olive oil

sea salt

freshly ground black pepper

2 oranges, skin and pith removed and finely sliced
  into rounds

4 cups (4 oz/125 g) baby spinach (English spinach)
  leaves

1 large, ripe avocado, pit and skin removed,
  cut into chunks

To make chickpea sprouts follow directions on page 21.

Mix together garlic, lemon and orange juices, cumin, cayenne and olive oil. Season to taste with salt and pepper and set aside. Place chickpea sprouts, orange slices, spinach leaves and avocado in a large bowl and gently toss together with dressing. Arrange decoratively on serving plates.

Note Baby spinach (English spinach) leaves are more intensely flavored and robust when dressed with an acidic dressing. Other types of baby spinach may collapse quickly when dressed.

Serves 4

SPROUTED GRAIN AND BEAN SALAD WITH SESAME LIME DRESSING

1 cup (3 oz/90 g) chickpea (garbanzo bean) sprouts

½ cup (1½ oz/45 g) wheat berry sprouts

½ cup (1½ oz/45 g) mixed bean sprouts (such as mung and lentil)

1 tablespoon dark (barley) miso

1 tablespoon lime juice

2 tablespoons cold-pressed sesame oil

freshly ground black pepper

½ oz (15 g) dried arame seaweed, soaked in tepid water for 30 minutes

4 teaspoons black or unhulled sesame seeds

4 scallions (shallots/spring onions), finely sliced on the diagonal

1 medium ripe avocado, pitted and peeled

Place sprouts in a colander and rinse under cold water, drain and toss to combine. In a large bowl, whisk together miso, lime juice, sesame oil and pepper to taste. Drain seaweed, squeeze out excess liquid and add to dressing. Toss through sprouts, ensuring they are well coated with dressing. Sprinkle sesame seeds and scallions on top and check seasoning. Serve with slices of avocado.

Serves 2–4

Note If you cannot purchase different sprouts or prefer to sprout them yourself, measure half the volumes given above for finished sprouts (they roughly double in volume when sprouted). Keep different types separate or, if you have plenty of sprouting space, mix them together. See page 21 for step by step sprouting directions.

Variation If you do not have any arame seaweed, substitute with 1–2 sheets of nori seaweed. Simply break up half the nori and toss through salad with sesame seeds and scallions. Break up the remaining nori and scatter over the top of the served salad. If you want the health benefits of fresh wheat grass but don't like to drink the juice, simply crop a handful of fresh wheat grass and toss it through this salad. You can grow wheat grass at home or buy it from health food stores.

ZUCCHINI, EGGPLANT AND BELL PEPPER RATATOUILLE

2 medium eggplant (aubergine)

sea salt

1 clove garlic, crushed

2 shallots (French shallots), finely diced

2 tablespoons white wine vinegar

¼ cup (2 fl oz/60 ml) extra virgin olive oil

freshly ground black pepper

4 medium zucchini (courgette), trimmed and
    chopped into ½ inch (1 cm) dice

4 plum (Roma) tomatoes, diced

1 red bell pepper (capsicum), seeded and
    cut into ½ cm (¼ inch) dice

½ cup (2 oz/60 g) pitted black olives, coarsely
    chopped

¼ cup chopped parsley

2 tablespoons snipped chives

2 tablespoons chopped mint

2 oz (60 g) pea shoots (optional)

Trim eggplant and cut into ¼ inch (½ cm) dice. Toss with salt and set aside for 20 minutes, then rinse and thoroughly pat dry with paper towels. Spread eggplant out on a dehydrator sheet or nonstick baking sheet and dry out either in a dehydrator or oven set to 110°F (55°C). Taste after 2 hours to check whether eggplant is soft and sweet. If not, continue to dehydrate. When eggplant is done, place garlic, shallot and vinegar in a bowl and whisk in olive oil. Season to taste with salt and pepper then toss through eggplant, zucchini, tomato, bell pepper and olive. Add herbs and check the seasoning. Serve as is, or on a bed of pea shoots.

Serves 4–6

Sweets

BANANA AND CINNAMON "ICE CREAM" WITH WALNUTS

4 large, ripe bananas
2 teaspoons pure vanilla extract (essence)
1 teaspoon ground cinnamon
1 tablespoon honey or pure maple syrup (optional)
¼ cup (1 oz/30 g) coarsely chopped walnuts

Peel and cut bananas into chunks. Spread chunks out flat on a sheet of parchment (baking) paper and freeze for 1 hour, or until solid. Remove from freezer and place in a food processor with vanilla and cinnamon. Process in bursts at first until bananas soften, then continuously until they become a creamy smooth consistency. Transfer to serving bowls, drizzle withhoney or maple syrup if using, then sprinkle with nuts. Serve immediately.

Serves 4

Note This is an excellent way to preserve and use surplus ripe bananas. If you know they will be used within a couple of weeks, first freeze the peeled chunks, then place them in a plastic bag in the freezer. If you have too many bananas for short-term use, they can be frozen whole, removed from the freezer 20 minutes before they're needed, and carefully peeled before proceeding with the recipe. Banana "ice cream" made from plain frozen bananas is a healthy treat for children who refuse fruit.

Vanilla extract is made from vanilla beans which, like raw honey, are briefly heat processed before curing. The flavor is incomparable, and the quantities used are so small that it is commonly accepted as a "raw" food.

Variation For a tropical version, omit the vanilla and cinnamon and replace with 1 tablespoon coconut cream per banana. Serve with fresh tropical fruits instead of nuts and honey or maple syrup. To keep ingredients on hand, freeze coconut cream in ice cube trays—each cube is about 1 tablespoon—and process with frozen banana.

COCONUT AND PINEAPPLE CREAM

1 small tropical pineapple
½ lime, plus 4–6 small wedges to serve
½ coconut, freshly grated, or ⅓ cup (3 fl oz/90 ml) coconut cream
1 bird's eye chili, seeded and very finely sliced
2 kaffir lime leaves, very finely sliced

Cut base and top off pineapple and sit it on its thickest end on a cutting board. Using a sharp knife, cut away skin, working your way from top to bottom in smooth, even strokes. Aim to make 8 even cuts so pineapple is octagonal in shape. Place pineapple on its side and cut into very thin slices, arranging slices in a single layer—like carpaccio—on serving plates as you go. Squeeze lime half over the pineapple slices, sprinkle with fresh coconut or drizzle coconut cream on top, then sprinkle with chili and lime leaves. Serve with a lime wedge.

Serves 4–6

Note Tropical pineapples are naturally very sweet and do not any further sweetener. To use regular pineapple, first taste for sweetness, then add a sprinkling of evaporated cane juice or a drizzle of pure maple syrup. For an authentically Asian flavor, you could use a small amount of grated palm sugar. The fresh sap from palm trees can be eaten immediately, but it quickly ferments, so to preserve it the sap is boiled, then evaporated for sale. It is therefore not a raw food unless freshly harvested.

COCONUT GRANITA WITH FRUIT SALAD

½ cup (4 fl oz/125 ml) coconut cream
½ cup (4 fl oz/125 ml) fresh sweet pineapple juice
raw honey (optional)
4 passionfruits, pulp removed
¼ small pineapple, peeled and cut into chunks
1 small mango, peeled and cut into chunks
2 kiwi fruits, peeled and cut into chunks
1 green coconut, flesh or "jelly" removed (optional)

Mix coconut cream and pineapple juice together and taste for sweetness. Add a little honey to sweeten if necessary. Pour into an ice cube tray and freeze until solid. When you are ready to serve, place passionfruit pulp in a bowl and gently toss with other tropical fruits. Place frozen coconut-pineapple cubes in a food processor and, ensuring the base of the machine is solid on the countertop, pulse a few times to break cubes down (this will be noisy). Continue to process until smooth and softened. Spoon fruit into chilled glasses or bowls, top with a scoop of coconut granita and coconut flesh if using.

Serves 4

Variation Other tropical fruits can be used in the fruit salad, such as papaya, star fruit (carambola), banana, litchi (lychee), mangosteen, rambutan, cherimoya (custard apple), sapote or soursop. Or, you can omit the tropical fruit salad and serve the granita with pomegranate seeds and blood orange segments.

PEACH MOUSSE WITH PISTACHIOS AND RASPBERRIES

2 cups (12 oz/375 g) dried peaches

2 cups (16 fl oz/500 ml) water

1 teaspoon raw honey

½ teaspoon ground cinnamon

¼ cup (1½ oz/45 g) almond meal

1–2 teaspoons rose water (optional)

¼ cup (1½ oz/45 g) coarsely chopped pistachios

1 cup (4 oz/125 g) raspberries

Soak peaches overnight in water at room temperature to reconstitute them. Next day, drain soaking liquid but do not discard it. Puree 1 cup (4 fl oz/125 ml) soaking liquid with peaches in a processor until very smooth (the remaining liquid can be drunk as peach-flavored water). Add honey, cinnamon, almond meal and rose water if using and blend until smooth. Spoon into small serving cups and refrigerate until set. Serve sprinkled with pistachios and raspberries on the side.

Serves 4

Note Commercial almond meal is usually made from blanched (not raw) almonds. If you want to be strictly raw, make your own almond meal from unpeeled or peeled almonds. Simply process in a blender, using the pulse button, until fine. Do not over process or the oils will be released.

Variation Dried apricots can be used in place of peaches, and fresh fruits other than raspberries could also be used. For a pretty garnish, scatter edible rose petals over the tops of the mousse, or toss with the raspberries.

SPICED STONE FRUITS MACERATED IN DESSERT WINE

4 medium peaches

4 apricots

4 nectarines

1 vanilla bean (pod), split lengthwise and seeds scraped

2 cinnamon sticks

1½ cups (12 fl oz/375 ml) dessert wine such as sauterne or late-picked riesling

½ cup (4 fl oz/125 ml) almond "yogurt" (see page 107) (optional), to serve

Cut fruit in half and remove the pits. Slice into slim wedges, place in a glass or ceramic bowl and toss gently with vanilla bean and seeds, and cinnamon sticks, taking care not to damage the fruit. Pour dessert wine over fruit, cover and set aside for a few hours at room temperature to macerate. Toss fruit gently from time to time. Using a slotted spoon, place fruit in serving glasses or cups, swirl liquid to distribute the vanilla seeds evenly and pour over fruit. Chill before serving with almond yogurt if desired.

Serves 4–6

Variation Mixed berry fruits may be tossed in champagne and served immediately, or citrus fruits such as orange and grapefruit also make a refreshing fruit maceration. Orange slices macerated with blueberries is especially good. Experiment with different sweet wines or, if you drink liqueurs, try macerating oranges in Grand Marnier instead of dessert wine. Because of its high alcohol content, use only a quarter of the volume as you would of dessert wine.

Sauces, dressings and condiments

BLACK OLIVE TAPENADE

1 cup (4 oz/125 g) pitted black olives

2 cloves garlic, crushed

1 bird's eye chili, seeded and finely chopped

2 tablespoons nonpareil (baby) capers, rinsed and patted dry

1 tablespoon lemon juice

⅔ cup (⅔ oz/20 g) chopped parsley

1 tablespoon finely chopped rosemary

1 tablespoon finely chopped thyme

½ cup (4 fl oz/125 ml) extra virgin olive oil, plus extra to preserve

sea salt

freshly ground black pepper

Place all ingredients with a pinch each of salt and pepper in a food processor and process until as coarse or fine as you prefer. Check seasoning and transfer to a ceramic dish or glass jar. Pack in tightly and cover with a film of olive oil to prevent air from contacting the surface. Cover and store in refrigerator for up to 1 week. Use as a dip for raw vegetables or as a base for salad dressing.

Makes about 1 cup (8 fl oz/250 ml)

CUCUMBER RAITA

2 English (hothouse) cucumbers or 4 Lebanese cucumbers, peeled and sliced paper-thin on the diagonal

sea salt

1 cup (8 fl oz/250 ml) water

½ cup (4 fl oz/125 ml) oat "yogurt" (see page 24)

1 teaspoon lemon juice

pinch of cayenne pepper

½ teaspoon ground cumin

1 tablespoon extra virgin olive oil

Place cucumber slices in a bowl. Dissolve 1 teaspoon salt in water then pour over cucumber slices. Allow to sit in the brine for 30 minutes. Drain and dry thoroughly with paper towels. Mix together oat yogurt, lemon juice, cayenne pepper, cumin and olive oil. Toss through cucumber and serve with a side of raw vegetables or salad greens.

Serves 4

DRIED TOMATO PASTE

30 plum (Roma) tomatoes
1 clove garlic, crushed
¼ cup (¼ oz/7 g) chopped parsley
¼ cup (¼ oz/7 g) chopped basil
2 tablespoons extra virgin olive oil, plus extra
    to preserve
sea salt
freshly ground black pepper

Bring a large pan of water to a boil and remove from heat. Place 6 tomatoes into water for up to 1 minute, then remove and chill under cold water. Return pan to heat and bring back to a boil. Meanwhile, peel each tomato using a small, sharp paring knife—skin should separate easily from flesh. Repeat with remaining tomatoes. Cut each tomato lengthwise into quarters and remove cores. Spread tomato quarters out, seed side up, on a dehydrator sheet or nonstick baking sheet and dry out either in a dehydrator or oven set to 110°F (55°C). The process may take 6–12 hours. Taste a piece of tomato from time to time—they should be intensely flavored with most moisture evaporated. When tomatoes are ready, puree to a paste with garlic, herbs and oil, and season to taste with salt and pepper. Transfer to a ceramic dish or glass jar, pack in tightly and cover with a film of olive oil to prevent air from contacting the surface. Cover and store in refrigerator for up to 1 week. Use as a dip, base for dressings, or spread over avocado or vegetables such as zucchini (courgettes) for an intense taste.

Makes about 1 cup (8 fl oz/250 ml)

Note Not all manufacturers of sun-dried tomatoes process their product at temperatures low enough to suit raw food followers. In most recipes that call for sun-dried tomatoes, the above method of dehydrating tomatoes, or the recipe for sun-drying on page 103 are preferable to using a product that may contain preservatives or be stored in an oil that is not cold-pressed. If you like the convenience and flavor of commercial sun-dried tomatoes, check the method of processing with the manufacturer of your preferred brand. Once dry, tomatoes have the advantage of being able to be stored at room temperature and there is no need for them to be stored in oil. To sun-dry your own tomatoes, you'll need long days of full sunshine and no humidity for tomatoes to dry at a rate that is faster than fermentation.

GARLIC-AND-ROSEMARY-INFUSED OLIVE OIL

1 cup (8 fl oz/250 ml) extra virgin olive oil
6 cloves garlic
1 large sprig rosemary
4 black peppercorns
½ teaspoon sea salt

Pour oil into a slim glass bottle. Gently smash garlic cloves, but do not break them up. Ease into bottle. Roll rosemary sprig in you hands to crush leaves gently and release aroma, then add to bottle. Lightly crush peppercorns and add along with salt. Secure bottle tightly, then gently turn upside down then right way up a few times to disperse ingredients. Place in refrigerator overnight for flavors to develop. Bring back to room temperature before using. The oil lasts well for up to a week and can be used in a dressing or alone over tomato, zucchini (courgette), mushroom, radish or bell pepper (capsicum).

Makes 1 cup (8 fl oz/250 ml)

Variation Instead of rosemary, use a few sprigs of pungent thyme and, for a more peppery oil, a split and mashed bird's eye chili.

PESTOS

Basil and pine nut
½ cup (4 fl oz/125 ml) extra virgin olive oil,
    plus extra to seal
2 cloves garlic
2 tablespoons pine nuts, soaked for 6 hours
4 cups (4 oz/125 g) basil leaves
sea salt
freshly ground black pepper

Cilantro and peanut
⅓ cup (3 fl oz/90 ml) extra virgin olive oil,
    plus extra to seal
2 cloves garlic
¼ cup (2 oz/60 g) peanuts
1 cup (1 oz/30 g) cilantro (fresh coriander) leaves
1 cup (1 oz/30 g) flat-leaf (Italian) parsley leaves
1 bird's eye chili, seeded and finely chopped
    (optional)
sea salt
freshly ground black pepper

Arugula and walnut
⅓ cup (3 fl oz/90 ml) extra virgin olive oil,
    plus extra to seal
2 cloves garlic
1 cup (4 oz/125 g) walnuts
3 cups (3 oz/90 g) chopped arugula (rocket) (do not
    use wild arugula)
sea salt
freshly ground black pepper

Tomato and almond
⅓ cup (3 fl oz/90 ml) extra virgin olive oil,
    plus extra to seal
4 cloves garlic
⅔ cup (3 oz/90 g) unpeeled almonds, soaked
    overnight
    and peeled
1 cup (7 oz/220 g) diced ripe tomato
1 cup (1 oz/30 g) basil leaves
1 bird's eye chili, seeded and finely chopped
    (optional)
sea salt
freshly ground black pepper

Common method to all types:
Place all ingredients of your chosen pesto in a
blender and season with salt and pepper (putting oil
in first will help the blender do its work). Blend until
as smooth or coarse as you prefer, check seasoning
and transfer to a ceramic bowl or glass jar and add
enough olive oil just to cover the surface. Cover and
store in refrigerator for up to 1 week. Use in salads,
with vegetables or as a spread.

Each recipe makes about 1–2 cups (8–16 fl oz/
250–500 ml)

Variation Other nut and leaf combinations could
include cashews, hazelnuts, mint or watercress.

PRESERVED LEMONS

6 organic lemons
9 tablespoons sea salt
2 bay leaves
2 cinnamon sticks
lemon juice to cover

Scrub lemons and cut lengthwise into quarters, but do not cut all the way through—lemon should still be joined at its base. Remove any visible seeds. Sprinkle 1 tablespoon salt in bottom of a sterilized 32-fl oz (1-L) jar. Pack remaining salt into center of each lemon and rub salt on outsides, then press each one back together so it looks whole again. Place lemons in jar, layering with bay leaves and cinnamon as you go. Press lemons down so some of the juice begins to run out. Wipe any salt from rim of jar and add enough extra lemon juice to cover lemons completely. Seal jar and set aside on a windowsill in the sun for first few days, shaking at least once a day, then set aside in a warm place to mature for 3–4 weeks more. The skin should be completely soft. Once open, store in refrigerator. To use, remove the amount you need, rinse well and finely chop, skin and all.

Makes 6 lemons

SAUERKRAUT

1 medium savoy cabbage
½ cup (4 oz/125 g) sea salt
1 tablespoon caraway seeds, a few juniper berries, or 2 bay leaves

Remove outer leaves from cabbage, rinse and set aside. Shred cabbage finely and pound together with salt to release its juices. Toss through caraway, juniper or bay if using and pack tightly into a stoneware or earthenware crock. Press down firmly and cover with reserved outer cabbage leaves. Place a plate on top and weigh it down with a 5 lb (2.5 kg) weight (you can use cans or a brick for this). Cover crock loosely with cheesecloth (muslin) then seal loosely with a lid. Set aside in a cool, dark place (not refrigerator) for a week or two until pleasantly fermented. Discard covering leaves and store sauerkraut in refrigerator. Rinse before using.

Makes About 1 lb (500 g), depending on the size of the cabbage

SUN-DRIED TOMATOES

12 plum (Roma) tomatoes
sea salt (optional)
whole garlic cloves (optional)
basil, thyme or rosemary (optional)
chili (optional)
freshly ground black pepper (optional)
olive oil

Cut tomatoes in half lengthwise, then either remove seeds or leave them in depending on your preference (if seeds are left in, tomatoes will need a longer drying time). Place tomato halves cut side down on a wire or bamboo rack and set in full sun for a few days to a week in a place safe from predators and insects. Bring tomatoes in at sunset so they do not pick up moisture in the evening air. Set out again each morning. When tomatoes are dry, layer in a sterilized jar with seasonings if you wish. Add enough olive oil to cover tomatoes, making sure there are no air pockets that may cause spoilage. The flavored oil can be used in dressings. If dried tomatoes are to be used within a few days, there is no need to preserve under oil.

Makes 24 halves

Note To oven-dry tomatoes, place racks of tomatoes in a dehydrator or oven set to 110°F (55°C) and dry for about 10–12 hours. Proceed as for sun-dried tomatoes.

Variation To sun-dry common white (field) mushrooms, wipe with a damp cloth, trim stalks and cut into ¼ inch (0.5 cm) slices. Lay out on wire racks and dry in the sun as for tomatoes. When completely crisp, store in an airtight container. Other vegetables that dry well include bell peppers (capsicum), green beans, leeks and sliced eggplant (aubergine). Simply wash and dry vegetables, ensuring they are unblemished and in peak condition. Dry thoroughly with paper towels, then thread them on cotton string and hang in an airy place until completely dry. Bell peppers and leeks will be reconstituted after an hour in cold water, while other vegetables will be ready in a matter of minutes.

Drinks

CAMPARI AND BLOOD ORANGE SLUSHIE

1⅔ cups (13 fl oz/400 ml) strained fresh blood
  orange juice
4–8 shots Campari
4 strips orange peel, tied into knots

Pour orange juice into an ice cube tray and freeze until solid. About 30 minutes before serving, place 4 serving glasses (such as martini), plus bowl and blade of a food processor, in the freezer to chill. To serve, place frozen orange juice cubes into chilled food processor bowl and, making sure its stable on countertop, pulse at first to break down cubes (it will be noisy and the processor may move). Then process rapidly until mixture is fine and powdery. Spoon mixture into serving glasses or bowls and pour Campari on top. Garnish with orange knots and serve immediately.

Serves 4

Variation Blood oranges have a short season, so you can either freeze juice in ice cube trays during a glut or use plain fresh orange, mandarin, tangelo or pink grapefruit juice instead. As a change from Campari, other orange-flavored spirits such as Cointreau or Grand Marnier may be substituted. Campari is produced using spirit maceration and water infusion of a secret, aromatic blend in neutral alcohol. It may not be strictly a raw food.

COOLING CUCUMBER AND MINT DRINK

2 English (hothouse) or 4 medium Lebanese
   cucumbers, peeled
2 teaspoons finely grated ginger
1 cup (8 fl oz/250 ml) water
1 cup (1 oz/30 g) mint leaves

Coarsely chop cucumbers and blend until smooth
with ginger, water and all but 2 mint sprigs. Pour over
ice, garnish with mint sprigs and serve immediately.

Serves 2

Note This drink is quick to make, has very little
energy and is an excellent way to cool down on a hot
summer day. The bitter skin is rich in chlorophyll, so
for an extra healthy boost the drink can also be made
using unpeeled cucumbers. For a very smooth result,
use a high-speed blender with good, sharp blades.

MANGO AND CARDAMOM LASSI

½ cup (2 oz/60 g) unpeeled almonds, soaked
   overnight in water and peeled

½ cup (4 fl oz/125 ml) water

½ teaspoon miso

1 large, ripe mango, peeled and pit removed and
   flesh cut into chunks

1 tablespoon raw honey

¼–½ teaspoon ground cardamom

8–10 ice cubes

2 teaspoons chopped pistachios (optional)

To make almond "yogurt", place almonds in a food
processor and process until fine. Add water and miso,
transfer to a ceramic dish and cover but do not seal
(cheesecloth/muslin works well). Set aside in a warm
place for up to 10 hours until your preferred level of
sourness is reached. Refrigerate until cold.

   To make drink, place chilled yogurt, mango flesh,
honey and ¼ teaspoon cardamom in a blender and
blend until smooth. Taste for cardamom and add a
little more if you prefer. Add ice cubes, blend again
to crush ice, then serve in chilled glasses. Sprinkle
with pistachios if using.

Serves 2

Note Lassi is a cooling Indian drink that may be either
sweet or savory. A simple savory version may be
seasoned with salt, pepper and ground cumin, while
sweet versions can include flower water. Once you've
mastered the almond yogurt base, experiment with
combinations you prefer. To speed fermentation of
the next batch, keep 1 tablespoon of ready yogurt
back and add it with miso to new ingredients. Yogurt
keeps well in the refrigerator for a few days.

INDEX

Ajo Blanco, 48

alcohol, 17

almond and grape soup, chilled, 48

apple

    celery and red apple salad with walnuts and "mayonnaise", 67

    green apple and radicchio salad with almond dressing, 68

artichoke

    artichoke, celery and pine nut salad with thyme and lemon dressing, 56

    arugula, walnut and Jerusalem artichoke soup, 50

    Jerusalem artichoke and spinach salad with hazelnut dressing, 71

arugula

    arugula, walnut and Jerusalem artichoke soup, 50

    black olive, fig and arugula salad, 60

asparagus spears with soy and sesame, 28

avocado

    avocado and corn soup with chili and cilantro, 51

    broccoli with green olive and avocado dip, 31

    spinach leaf, orange and avocado salad with chickpea sprouts, 83

baby leeks with green olive and caper tapenade, 59

banana and cinnamon "ice cream" with walnuts, 88

beans, 12

    broccolini with fermented black beans, 63

    cucumber and long beans in chili peanut dressing, 34

    green and yellow, with walnut sauce, 38

    sprouted grain and bean salad with sesame lime dressing, 84

beet and carrot salad with walnuts, 60

Belgian endive cups with gremolata, 30

bell peppers

    celery root rémoulade with red bell pepper and chervil, 33

    rainbow bell pepper salad with capers and preserved lemon, 82

    zucchini, eggplant and bell pepper ratatouille, 87

bircher muesli with strawberries and hazelnuts, 22

black olive, fig and arugula salad, 60

black olive tapenade, 96

blenders, 18

bok choy with Asian mushrooms marinated in ginger soy dressing, 62

breakfast, 22–7

broccoli with green olive and avocado dip, 31

broccolini with fermented black beans, 63

cabbage (red and green) and kale coleslaw, 80

campari and blood orange slushie, 104

capers

    baby leeks with green olive and caper tapenade, 59

    rainbow bell pepper salad with capers and preserved lemon, 82

carrot

    beet and carrot salad with walnuts, 60

    carrot stick salad with cilantro and chili, 64

cauliflower soup, creamed, 55

celery

    artichoke, celery and pine nut salad with thyme and lemon dressing, 56

    celery and red apple salad with walnuts and "mayonnaise", 67

    celery root rémoulade with red bell pepper and chervil, 33

    mixed marinated olives with herbs and celery, 40

    pistachio, celery and cucumber salad with dates, 78

charmoula, zucchini strips with, 47

cheesecloth, 18

chilled cucumber soup with red radishes, 52

coconuts, 12

    coconut and pineapple cream, 91

    coconut granita with fruit salad, 91

coleslaw, red and green cabbage and kale, 80

compote of dried fruits with oat "yogurt", 24

condiments, 96–103

cooling cucumber and mint drink, 106

corn and avocado soup with chili and cilantro, 51

creamed cauliflower soup, 55

cucumber

    chilled cucumber soup with red radishes, 52

    cooling cucumber and mint drink, 106

    cucumber and long beans in chili peanut dressing, 34

    cucumber raita, 96

    pistachio, celery and cucumber salad with dates, 78

cutting boards, 18

daikon, radish and kohlrabi salad, 79

dates, pistachio, celery and cucumber salad with, 78

dehydrator, 18

dolmas, 46

dressings, 96–103

dried fruit, 12

    compote of, with oat "yogurt", 24

dried tomato paste, 98

drinks, 104–7

edible flowers, 12

eggplant, zucchini and bell pepper ratatouille, 87

equipment, 18–20

fennel

    fennel carpaccio with green olives, 37

    pink grapefruit, fennel and red onion salad, 76

figs

    black olive, fig and arugula salad, 60

    fig and melon in port wine, 37

flower waters, 12

food processor, 18

freezing fresh foods, 9

fresh produce, 11

fruit and nut granola with pepita "milk", 25

fruit salad

    coconut granita with, 91

    melon, with mint, 27

granola, fruit and nut, with pepita "milk", 25

grapefruit (pink), fennel and red onion salad, 76

grasses, 12

green and yellow beans with walnut sauce, 38

green apple and radicchio salad with almond dressing, 68

green olives

    baby leeks with green olive and caper tapenade, 59

    broccoli with green olive and avocado dip, 31

    fennel carpaccio with, 37

gremolata, Belgian endive cups with, 30

herbs, 12

honey, 14

hummus, vegetable crudités with, 45

"ice cream", banana and cinnamon, with walnuts, 88

Japanese vegetable slicer, 18

Jerusalem artichoke

    arugula, Jerusalem artichoke and walnut soup, 50

    Jerusalem artichoke and spinach salad with hazelnut

        dressing, 71

juicers, 18

knives, 20

kohlrabi, radish and daikon salad, 79

lassi, mango and cardamom, 107

leeks (baby) with green olive and caper tapenade, 59

legumes, 12

lemon

macerated lemon and tomato salad, 72

preserved, 102

rainbow bell pepper salad with capers and preserved lemon, 82

long beans and cucumber in chili peanut dressing, 34

macerated lemon and tomato salad, 72

mandoline, 18

mango and cardamom lassi, 107

melon

fig and, in port wine, 37

fruit salad with mint, 27

mint

cooling cucumber and mint drink, 106

melon fruit salad with, 27

tomato and mint "gazpacho", 55

miso, 14

mixed marinated olives with herbs and celery, 40

mousse, peach, with pistachios and raspberries, 92

muesli

bircher, with strawberries and hazelnuts, 22

honey and almond milk, with, 27

mushrooms, 14

bok choy with Asian mushrooms marinated in ginger soy dressing, 62

tomato-band-basil-stuffed, 42

muslin, 18

mustard, 14

nuts, 14

spicy mixed, 41

oils, 15

olive oil, garlic-and-rosemary-infused, 99

olives

mixed marinated with herbs and celery, 40

orange, red onion and olive salad, 72

orange

campari and blood orange slushie, 104

orange, red onion and olive salad, 72

spinach leaf, orange and avocado salad with chickpea sprouts, 83

organic produce, 9–10

oven-dried tomatoes, 103

oven thermometer, 20

peach mousse with pistachios and raspberries, 92

pear, walnut and bitter greens salad, 75

peeling, 11

pepper, 15

pestos, 101

pine nuts

artichoke, celery and pine nut salad with thyme and lemon dressing, 56

vine leaves stuffed with currants, Swiss chard and, 46

pineapple and coconut cream, 91

pink grapefruit, fennel and red onion salad, 76

pistachios

peach mousse with pistachios and raspberries, 92

pistachio, celery and cucumber salad with dates, 78

port wine, fig and melon with, 37

preserved lemons, 102

radicchio and green apple salad with almond dressing, 68

radishes

chilled cucumber soup with red radishes, 52

radish, kohlrabi and daikon salad, 79

raw foods, definition, 9

red bell pepper, celery root rémoulade and chervil with, 33

red onions

orange, red onion and olive salad, 72

pink grapefruit, fennel and red onion salad, 76

salad leaves, 15
  pear, walnut and bitter greens salad, 75
salads, 56–87
sauces, 96–103
sauerkraut, 102
scales, 20
sea salt, sun-dried, 17
seaweed, 15
sesame, 15
  asparagus spears with soy and sesame, 28
snacks, 28–47
soups, 48–55
soy sauce, 15–17
  asparagus spears with soy and sesame, 28
Spanish chilled almond and grape soup, 48
spiced stone fruits macerated in dessert wine, 95
spiced vegetable crisps, 41
spices, 12
spicy mixed nuts, 41
spinach
  Jerusalem artichoke and spinach salad with hazelnut
    dressing, 71
  spinach leaf, orange and avocado salad with chickpea
    sprouts, 83
sprouted grain and bean salad with sesame lime dressing, 84
sprouting, 21
sprouts, 15
starters, 28–47
stone fruits, spiced, macerated in dessert wine, 95
sun-dried sea salt, 17
sun-dried tomatoes, 103
sweetners, 17
sweets, 88–95

tahini, 15
tomato
  dried tomato paste, 98
  macerated lemon and tomato salad, 72

sun- or oven-dried, 103
tomato-and-basil-stuffed mushrooms, 42
tomato and mint "gazpacho", 55

vegetable crisps, spiced, 41
vegetable crudités with hummus, 45
vegetable scrubbing brushes, 20
vegetables, 56–87
vine leaves stuffed with pine nuts, currants and Swiss chard,
  46
vinegar, 17

walnuts
  arugula, walnut and Jerusalem artichoke soup, 50
  banana and cinnamon "ice cream" with, 88
  beet and carrot salad with walnuts, 60
  celery and red apple salad with walnuts and "mayonnaise",
    67
  green and yellow beans with walnut sauce, 38
  pear, walnut and bitter greens salad, 75
washing, 11
water, 17
wine, 15

yoghurt
  almond, 107
  compote of dried fruits with oat "yogurt", 24
  nondairy, 24

zucchini, eggplant and bell pepper ratatouille, 87
zucchini strips with charmoula, 47

WEIGHTS AND MEASUREMENTS

The conversions given in the recipes in this book are approximate. Whichever system you use, remember to follow it consistently, to ensure that the proportions are consistent throughout a recipe.

Weights

Imperial	Metric
1/3 oz	10 g
1/2 oz	15 g
3/4 oz	20 g
1 oz	30 g
2 oz	60 g
3 oz	90 g
4 oz (1/4 lb)	125 g
5 oz (1/3 lb)	150 g
6 oz	180 g
7 oz	220 g
8 oz (1/2 lb)	250 g
9 oz	280 g
10 oz	300 g
11 oz	330 g
12 oz (3/4 lb)	375 g
16 oz (1 lb)	500 g
2 lb	1 kg
3 lb	1.5 kg
4 lb	2 kg

Volume

Imperial	Metric	Cup
1 fl oz	30 ml	
2 fl oz	60 ml	1/4
3 fl oz	90 ml	1/3
4 fl oz	125 ml	1/2
5 fl oz	150 ml	2/3
6 fl oz	180 ml	3/4
8 fl oz	250 ml	1
10 fl oz	300 ml	1 1/4
12 fl oz	375 ml	1 1/2
13 fl oz	400 ml	1 2/3
14 fl oz	440 ml	1 3/4
16 fl oz	500 ml	2
24 fl oz	750 ml	3
32 fl oz	1 L	4

Oven temperature guide

The Celsius (°C) and Fahrenheit (°F) temperatures in this chart apply to most electric ovens. Decrease by 25°F or 10°C for a gas oven or refer to the manufacturer's temperature guide. For temperatures below 325°F (160°C), do not decrease the given temperature.

Oven description	°C	°F	Gas Mark
Cool	110	225	1/4
	130	250	1/2
Very slow	140	275	1
	150	300	2
Slow	170	325	3
Moderate	180	350	4
	190	375	5
Moderately hot	200	400	6
Fairly hot	220	425	7
Hot	230	450	8
Very hot	240	475	9
Extremely hot	250	500	10

Useful conversions

1 tablespoon	1/2 oz	15 g
1 1/2 tablespoons	3/4 oz	20 g
2 tablespoons	1 oz	30 g
3 tablespoons	1 1/2 oz	45 g

1/4 teaspoon	1.25 ml
1/2 teaspoon	2.5 ml
1 teaspoon	5 ml
1 Australian tablespoon	20 ml (4 teaspoons)
1 UK/US tablespoon	15 ml (3 teaspoons)